Activities for the Internet

A Mastery Course

Dr. Joe Jernigan, Assistant Professor of Educational Technology
The University of Texas at Arlington
Arlington, Texas

Joyce Perkins
Hardin-Jefferson High School
Sour Lake, Texas

Reviewers:

Kay Franklin
Canyon High School
New Braunfels, Texas

Kay Cade Pleasant
Tyler ISD
Tyler, Texas

Jamye Swinford
Crane High School
Crane, Texas

JOIN US ON THE INTERNET

WWW: http://www.thomson.com
EMAIL: findit@kiosk.thomson.com   A service of I(T)P®

South-Western Educational Publishing

an International Thomson Publishing company I(T)P®

Cincinnati • Albany, NY • Belmont, CA • Bonn • Boston • Detroit • Johannesburg • London • Madrid
Melbourne • Mexico City • New York • Paris • Singapore • Tokyo • Toronto • Washington

Managing Editor: Janie F. Schwark
Editor: Becky E. Peveler
Marketing Manager: John Wills
Development Services: FSCreations, Inc.
Production Services: FSCreations, Inc. and Mary Hartkemeyer
Internal/Cover Design: Ann Small
Internal/Cover Photo: Marjory Dressler
Manufacturing Coordinator: Mardell Toomey

I(T)P

South-Western Educational Publishing is a division of International Thomson Publishing, Inc. The ITP logo is a registered trademark used herein under license by South-Western Educational Publishing.

Preface

Our lives continue to change in many ways with the tremendous impact of the Internet, the World Wide Web, and telecommunications. Business we once handled by visits, calls, or mail to stores and offices, we now conduct on the computer via the Internet. The Internet has a wealth of information that you can access from a classroom, your home, or work. And you can communicate with anyone around the world when you learn to use the Internet.

Activities for the Internet: A Mastery Course will help you to continue your exploration of the Internet with more in-depth activities. After exploring the Internet for just a very few hours, you will develop advanced telecommunications skills and thus be better prepared for the twenty-first century. Your journey will provide educational experiences, challenges, and excitement; new friendships; and new knowledge and skills for success at school, at work, and at home.

ORGANIZATION OF THE BOOK

Activities for the Internet: A Mastery Course is divided into three parts:

Part 1—Introduction

Part 1 provides an overview of the primary tools for exploring the Internet. You can use the Introduction to review basic terminology related to the Internet and the World Wide Web. Whether you will be using Netscape Navigator or Microsoft Internet Explorer, you will find the step-by-step instructions to explore on the Internet. After you refer to the Introduction, you will be ready to explore on your own in the activities.

Part 2—Activities and Portfolio Project

Part 2 has twenty independent Internet activities and a portfolio project that often involve individual and team tasks. The activities provide general steps to guide you as you explore the Internet to complete the in-depth activities. Each activity will challenge you to conduct relevant research on the Internet to meet the objectives of each activity, and your work for each activity will include business applications. As you complete each activity, you will have an opportunity to:

- Learn and apply advanced telecommunications skills.
- Gain new knowledge about personal, local, state, national, and international business topics.
- Develop critical thinking, communication, research, and teamwork skills as you apply emerging technologies in workplace business situations.

- Create and build a portfolio with samples that demonstrate the telecommunications and applications software skills you have mastered over time.

Part 3—Glossary

Part 3 lists terms and definitions to help you expand your vocabulary. Access the glossary whenever you need to review the definition of an Internet-related term that you may have seen elsewhere in the book.

FEATURES OF THE BOOK

Take time now to notice these features in *Activities for the Internet: A Mastery Course:*

- **Net Web Wisdom**, in the form of marginal notes throughout the book, provides answers to FAQs about the Internet and the World Wide Web.
- **Notes** provide hints to help you explore successfully.
- **Screen illustrations** that you may encounter on your journey are included. Because the Internet is ever-changing, some of the screen illustrations may look different on your screen.
- **Objectives** identify what you should learn during your exploration for each activity.
- **Feedback questions** in each of the twenty activities guide your exploration.
- **Applications** within each activity direct you to create documents using word processing, spreadsheet, database, telecommunications, desktop publishing, presentation, and other applications software.

ACKNOWLEDGMENTS

Writing this book was truly a team effort. Our many thanks to:

- Becky Peveler, our developmental editor at South-Western Educational Publishing, who believed in us through this fast and furious project.
- Nina Watson, our editor at FSCreations, Inc., who did an extraordinary job of deciphering our e-mail and learning along with us. Because of the capability of telecommunications, almost all our work was sent to one another via e-mail.

Special thanks to our reviewers for their contributions:

- Kay Franklin, Canyon High School, New Braunfels, Texas
- Kay Cade Pleasant, Tyler ISD, Tyler, Texas
- Jamye Swinford, Crane High School, Crane, Texas

Finally, from Joe, thanks to those who had to put up with me during this project: my best friend, Archie Bailey; my colleagues at The University of Texas at Arlington; and the one who sacrificed most of his time with me, my dog Ed Earl.

From Joyce, a huge hug to my family: Mark and Justin. Even though I was busy with all the other things at home, at school, or with student council, my family supported me throughout the work on this project. Also a big thanks for the years of support to my extended online family and my colleagues at Lesley College and Hardin-Jefferson High School.

We welcome an e-mail message to let us know your reactions to this book or your thoughts about your favorite activity. You may send an e-mail message to either of us at these addresses:

Joe Jernigan   joej@tenet.edu   or   jernigan@uta.edu

Joyce Perkins   jperkins@tenet.edu

As you explore the Internet, concentrate on learning all you can about the world of telecommunications. As a result, you will master advanced telecommunications skills and knowledge for workplace success.

Joe Jernigan

Joyce Perkins

Contents

Part 3   Glossary   91

Index   99

Acknowledgments

For permission to reproduce the screen captures on the indicated pages, acknowledgment is made to the following:

Page	Source
7, 15, 62, 79	Netscape Communications Corporation has not authorized, sponsored, or endorsed, or approved this publication and is not responsible for its content. Netscape and the Netscape Communications Corporate Logos, are trademarks and trade names of Netscape Communications Corporation. All other product names and/or logos are trademarks of their respective owners.
8	Microsoft Corporation has not authorized, sponsored, or endorsed, or approved this publication and is not responsible for its content. Microsoft is a registered trademark of Microsoft Corporation.
7, 9	U.S. Census Bureau
26	Mecklermedia Corporation, 20 Ketchum Street, Westport, CT 06880; (201)341-2802; info@mecklermedia.com; http://www.iworld.com. All rights reserved. Reprinted with permission.
29	TENET
32	California State University, Fullerton Web Site
35	National Center for Education Statistics
35	National Center for Education Statistics and Youth Indicators
38	Business Professionals of America
39	Future Business Leaders—Phi Beta Lambda
41, 42	College Funding Company
43	Federal Information Exchange, Inc.
46	Kiwi Shoe Care Network
50	BenefitsLink™

Page	Source
56	Symmetry Software
59, 60	The Homebuyer's Fair, LLC
66	Hitchhikers Internet Services
69	Office of Management and Budget
69	U.S. Department of Commerce
72	Ainsworth Computer Seminar
74	Web66 at University of Minnesota
75	Eisenhower High School, Houston, Texas
78	Text and artwork copywrite 1996 by YAHOO!, INC. All rights reserved. YAHOO! and the YAHOO! logo are trademarks of YAHOO!, INC.
82	Bay Networks
85	Warp, Ltd.
87	Reproduced with the permission of Digital Equipment Corporation. AltaVista and the AltaVista logo and the Digital logo are trademarks of Digital Equipment Corporation.

JOIN US ON THE INTERNET

WWW: **http://www.thomson.com**
E-MAIL: **findit@kiosk.thomson.com**

South-Western Educational Publishing is a partner in *thomson.com*, an on-line portal for the products, services, and resources available from International Thomson Publishing (ITP). Through our site, users can search catalogs, examine subject-specific resource centers, and subscribe to electronic discussion lists.

South-Western Educational Publishing is also a reseller of commercial software products. See our printed catalog or view this page at:

http://www.swpco.com/swpco/comp_ed/com_sft.html

For information on our products visit our World Wide Web site at:

http://www.swpco.com/swpco.html

To join the South-Western Computer Education discussion list, send an e-mail message to: **majordomo@list.thomson.com**. Leave the subject field blank, and in the body of your message key: SUBSCRIBE SOUTH-WESTERN-COMPUTER-EDUCATION <your e-mail address>.

A service of $I\textcircled{T}P$®

One Two Three

1 2 3

Introduction

▶ OVERVIEW

Do you remember when you made a phone call to communicate with someone, you placed a stamp on your mail, you went to a library to conduct research, you visited a retail store to shop for clothing or books, you visited a travel agency to arrange a trip, or you learned about the weather by listening to weather reports?

Why is the Internet so important to the world?

Now our world is so very different. You can conduct much of your daily business on the computer. E-mail addresses and World Wide Web sites are everywhere: in newspapers, magazines, and journals; on business cards and letterhead; on television and radio commercials; on billboards; on the local and national news; and on junk mail. Many of your friends may even have an e-mail address.

What is the Internet?

Your teacher will discuss the communications software you will be using.

You have undoubtedly heard about the Internet, the information superhighway, or surfing the Net. The Internet, also called the Net, consists of people, information, and millions of interconnected computer networks throughout the world. Most businesses and homes are connected to the Internet via an **Internet service provider** (ISP) such as America Online, CompuServe, Prodigy, or a local provider. For a monthly fee, an ISP will provide full Internet access through a phone line. All you need is a computer, communications software, and a modem with a phone line.

If you have ever been to a library, you have seen the physical equivalent of the Internet. A library contains thousands of books, each stored on a specific shelf in a specific section of the library. Each book has a unique number, or address, assigned to it that tells you exactly where you can find the book. Each item on the Internet also has a unique address that allows you to access specific files.

Your browser will help you find information on the Internet

Special software programs called **browsers** help you find information on the Internet. Since the information on the Internet is **hypertext-driven**, you can jump from a word, graphic, or phrase to another section in a document or to a different document via a **hypertext link**.

Internet Addresses

When you are connected to the Internet, you are identified by a unique address. This address allows you to access information, and others may send information to your address. An Internet address may be numeric, alphabetic, or a combination of numbers and letters. Internet e-mail addresses always use lowercase letters with no spaces.

All Internet e-mail addresses have several parts, separated by the @ (pronounced *at*) symbol. The **username** identifies the specific person at that site. The **domain** and **subdomain** identify the computer where the user is working. The last three letters, called the **domain extension** or the **top-level domain**, refer to the top domain name for the network. Common domain extensions are shown in Figure 1-1 on page 4.

Figure 1-1
Common Domain
Extensions

Domain Extension	Description	Example of Internet Address
.com	Commercial Service	billg@microsoft.com (Bill Gates, CEO of Microsoft Corporation)
.edu	Education or Education-related Organization	jperkins@tenet.edu (Joyce Perkins, a coauthor of this text)
.gov	Government	president@whitehouse.gov (The President of the United States)
.mil	Military	shorta@karpeles.ims.disa.mil (General Alonzo Short, head of the Defense Information Systems Agency)
.net	Network Provider	@fuse.net (an Internet service provider via Cincinnati Bell Telephone)
.org	Organization	@nassp.org (National Association of Secondary School Principals)

Each hypertext link has a unique URL.

Files on the Internet have a similar kind of location number, or address, called a **Universal Resource Locator**, or **URL** (pronounced *Earl*). Each hypertext link is connected to a unique URL, telling the browser where to find that particular document. URL names look different than normal Internet names. These long names are seen everywhere in hyperspace. The following are some examples:

http://www.disney.com/   Disneyland
http://www.whitehouse.gov/   White House
http://cdsweb.u-strasbg.fr/~heck/sf.htm/ The Star's Family of Astronomy
http://fi-www.arc.nasa.gov/fia/projects/
   bayes-group/Atlas/Mars/   Atlas of Mars

Many URLs begin with http:.

You must type the URL exactly correct, with no spaces in the address. Since URLs are also case sensitive, you must type uppercase or lowercase letters exactly as shown.

What is the World Wide Web?

The **World Wide Web**, also known as the WWW, is a hypermedia system that lets you browse through lots of information on the Internet. You can find information on just about any topic. If you enter the URL for the information you want to access on the Internet, your browser will jump or **link** immediately to that location. Or, from a browser, you can jump easily from a hypertext link in one document to another page in the same document or to a different site and other documents all over the world. By exploring link after link, you create a web of connections.

Will you be using a graphical browser or a text browser?

A **graphical browser** (often called a GUI or a graphical user interface and pronounced *gooey*) allows you to access text, color, video, sound, and multimedia presentations on the Internet. Popular graphical browsers are Netscape Navigator (or Netscape) and Microsoft Internet Explorer (or Explorer). A **text browser**, such as Lynx, provides access to only text (or words) on the Internet. To access graphics or pictures using Lynx, you must download the pages and then use a graphics viewer.

The hypertext links on home pages and web pages are highlighted, underlined, or in a different color.

Documents on the World Wide Web are referred to as either home pages or web pages. A **home page** is the main page for a web site. You can compare a home page to a menu, since the home page will often identify links to other pages at this site. A **web page** (or **page**) contains the information for a hypertext link. Home pages and web pages may have numerous links. As an example, Disneyland has only one home page (**http://www.disney.com**) with many hypertext links, each with a unique URL (such as the Disney Store at **http://store.disney.com/** or Disney Publishing at **http://www.disney.com/DisneyBooks/**).

Some HTML documents have *.html* or *.htm* at the end of the URL.

With the variety of computer applications, all documents are not created the same way. For example, some documents could have been created using WordPerfect, while others may be in Microsoft Word. Some documents are in a DOS format, while others are Macintosh documents. For everyone in the world to read each other's files, HTML was developed. **HTML**, or HyperText Markup Language, refers to the embedded instructions within regular text. These instructions allow each browser to display a document clearly on your screen.

Tips for Getting Started

To help you learn about the Internet, follow these tips:

- Log on to the Internet daily.
- Schedule an uninterrupted block of time to explore.
- Be responsible for acceptable computer use and for your teacher's account.
- Keep a pen or pencil and a spiral notebook or notepad nearby to record important information.
- Get into the habit of keeping a journal of your online activities, critical commands or steps you most often use, and e-mail addresses of users with whom you would like to communicate.
- After you are off-line, get into the habit of reviewing what you learned during that session.
- Always prepare for your next online session. Think about where you will want to try to find the information you are looking for or how you can make your online session more productive.

Responsible behavior is critical when you access the Internet. Your teacher will discuss the acceptable use policy you must follow.

The Introduction will help you get started using the Internet.

As you complete the activities in this book, you will become comfortable with the Internet. Your journey will provide educational experiences, challenges, and excitement; new friendships; and new knowledge and skills for success at school, at work, and at home. You will learn how to use the Internet to gain information about the diverse cultures of the world, to conduct research, to try software, to communicate with others, to arrange travel plans, to discuss your favorite topic, to look at fashion designs before they arrive at your local department store, to explore the world, and on and on.

By now you should be familiar with terms such as Internet, ISP, browsers, hypertext link, address, URL, WWW, graphical browser, text browser, HTML, home page, *and* web page (or page). *If you aren't, please review the material on pages 3–6 before you begin working at the computer in the next section.*

► LAUNCHING YOUR BROWSER

Remember that your browser helps you find information on the Internet. The steps to launch your browser will vary with the communications software that you will be using. No matter what communications software you will use, however, you will learn quickly as part of your daily routine how to launch your browser.

Important: The step-by-step instructions in this book are based on Netscape Navigator 3.0 and Microsoft Internet Explorer 3.0. If you are using an earlier or more recent version of the software, some steps may differ depending on the activity.

If you are using Netscape Navigator for Windows or for a Macintosh computer, follow these steps to launch your browser:

1. Start the Netscape Navigator software. The Netscape Navigator home page will appear unless you set a different start page. If the Netscape Navigator home page did not appear, type **http://home.netscape.com/** in the Location box.
    Note: The Location box is located near the top of the window. The name of the box changes when your browser links to sites. You will see these names for the Location box: *Netsite:, Go to:, and Location.*

2. Your screen should be similar to the Netscape Navigator home page in Figure 1-2 on page 7. Realize that the content on a web page may change at any time.

    The **status indicator** at the bottom of the screen animates to show the progress of the current operation. The URLs for each hypertext link will appear in this area. The **toolbar buttons** at the top of the screen activate Netscape Navigator features. Click on the buttons to revisit pages, reload pages, load images, open locations, print pages, find text, and stop transfers in progress. The **directory buttons** under the toolbar buttons bring pages whose information helps you browse the Internet, such as new sites and "cool" sites.

3. Because most documents are larger than what appears on your screen, use the scroll bar to move up and down the pages to read the entire document.
    Note: Get into the habit of scrolling the home page of each site you visit so you will know the hypertext links on the home page.

4. In the Location box, type **http://www.census.gov/** and press ENTER/ RETURN. You will be connected to the web page for the U.S. Census Bureau as shown in Figure 1-3 on page 7.

Since all graphical browsers have similar features, you will be able to use different browsers after you learn about Netscape Navigator or Microsoft Internet Explorer.

Netscape

Practice these steps to become comfortable with launching Netscape Navigator and linking to other pages and sites. When you are ready to exit Netscape Navigator, see "Exiting Your Computer Session" on page 22.

Figure 1-2
Netscape Navigator Home
Page

Toolbar
Buttons

Directory
Buttons

Hypertext
Link

Status
Indicator

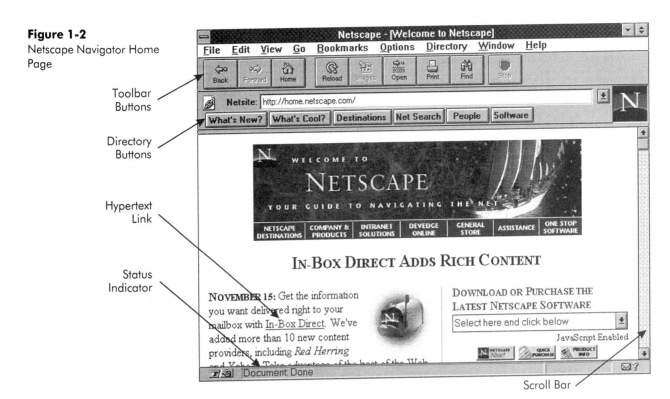

Scroll Bar

Figure 1-3
U.S. Census Bureau Home
Page from Netscape

Important: As you explore the Internet, always remember to leave an objectionable site quickly by clicking the Home button. You will immediately return to the home page set up for your browser.

5. *Optional:* Click on the Print button to print the home page that appears on your screen.
   Note: The default is set to print all the pages in the document, but you can specify the pages that you want to print in the Print dialog box.

6. Read the U.S. Census Bureau home page, and click on any hypertext link.

7. Practice using hypertext by selecting several more links.

8. Click on the Back button, and retrace your steps until you reach the U.S. Census Bureau home page.

9. Click on the Forward button to retrace the links you chose earlier.

10. Click the Home button to go to the Netscape Navigator home page.

Explorer

Practice these steps to become comfortable with launching Explorer and linking to other pages and sites. When you are ready to exit the browser, see "Exiting Your Computer Session" on page 22.

If you are using Microsoft Internet Explorer for Windows or for a Macintosh computer, follow these steps to launch your browser:

1. Start the Microsoft Internet Explorer software. The Microsoft Internet Explorer home page will appear unless you set a different start page. If the Explorer home page did not appear, type **http://home.microsoft.com/** in the Address box near the top of the window.

2. Your screen should be similar to the Microsoft Internet Explorer home page in Figure 1-4. Realize that the content on a web page may change at any time.

Figure 1-4
Microsoft Internet Explorer Home Page

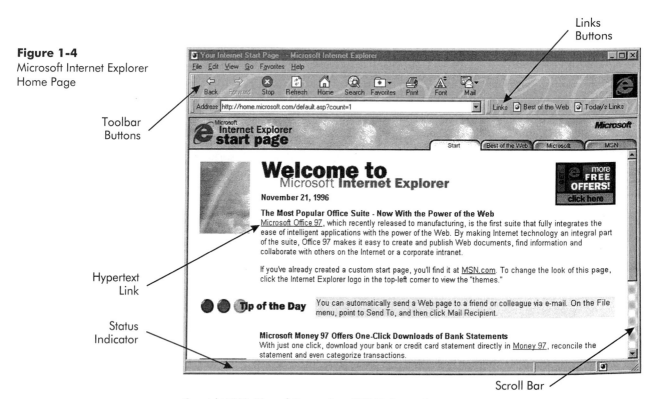

The **status indicator** at the bottom of the screen animates to show the progress of the current operation. The URLs for each hypertext link will appear in this area. The **toolbar buttons** at the top of the screen activate Explorer features. Click on the buttons to revisit pages, refresh pages, load images, open locations, print pages, search for text, and stop transfers in progress. The **links buttons** next to the Address box bring pages whose information helps you browse the Internet, such as "Best of the Web" and "Today's Links."

3. Because most documents are larger than what appears on your screen, use the scroll bar to move up and down the pages to read the entire document.
   Note: Get into the habit of scrolling the home page of each site you visit so you will know the hypertext links on the home page.

4. In the Address box, type **http://www.census.gov/** and press ENTER/RETURN. You will be connected to the web page for the U.S. Census Bureau as shown in Figure 1-5.

Figure 1-5
U.S. Census Bureau Home Page from Explorer

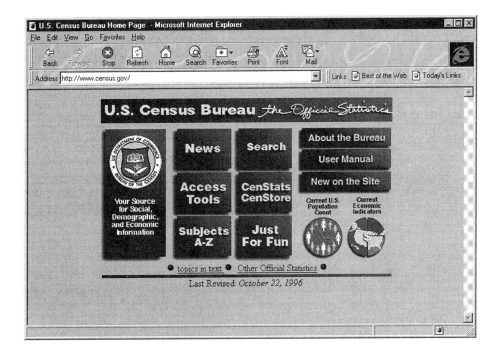

Important: As you explore the Internet, always remember to leave an objectionable site quickly by clicking the Home button. You will immediately return to the home page set up for your browser.

5. *Optional:* Click on the Print button to print the home page that appears on your screen.
   Note: The default is set to print all the pages in the document, but you can specify the pages that you want to print in the Print dialog box.

6. Read the U.S. Census Bureau home page, and click on any hypertext link.

7. Practice using hypertext by selecting several more links.

8. Click on the Back button, and retrace your steps until you reach the U.S. Census Bureau home page.

9. Click on the Forward button to retrace the links you chose earlier.

10. Click the Home button to go to the Internet Explorer home page.

ACCESSING ONLINE HELP

Online help provides instructions to perform various tasks.

Whenever you need to learn or review the steps to perform various tasks, you can access online help. Online help provides definitions, instructions, and perhaps a tutorial to help you become familiar with the functions of the software.

Netscape

If you are using Netscape Navigator, follow these steps to access online help:

1. If you need help at any time when you are using Netscape Navigator, choose the **Help** menu. Note the various options.

2. To access descriptions of terms and instructions to perform a specific task, choose *Handbook*.

3. Scroll down the page. Explore the tutorial options if you want to review the basics of Netscape Navigator. If you want to search for help on a particular topic, continue scrolling to the *Index*. By choosing the initial letter of the topic in which you need help, Netscape Navigator will link immediately to the items in the Index. Continue using hypertext links to find the information you need.

4. To exit Help and to continue browsing, click on the Back button or choose to go to a specific page.

Explorer

If you are using Microsoft Internet Explorer, follow these steps to access online help:

1. If you need help at any time when you are using Explorer, choose the **Help** menu. Note the various options.

2. To access descriptions of terms and instructions to perform a specific task, choose *Help Topics*. If you want to search for help on a particular topic, continue scrolling through the list. Click on a topic about which you want to learn more.

3. Choose *Web Tutorial* if you want to review the basics of Explorer or if you want to complete lessons. Go to URL: **http://www.msn.com/ tutorial/default.html** if the *Web Tutorial* is not available in the **Help** menu. Continue using hypertext links to find the information you need.

4. To exit Help and to continue browsing, click on the Back button or choose to go to a specific page.

FINDING FILES WITH SEARCH ENGINES

Searching for information takes time and patience.

When you don't know a specific URL for the information you need, you can use a search engine. A **search engine** allows you to search for information on a particular topic on the Internet. For example, you could search for the words *space shuttle*. A search engine will access the Internet and show you a list of documents containing the words *space* and *shuttle*. You would then browse the documents to find the information that interests you. Examples of popular search engines are Yahoo, AltaVista, Lycos, Magellan, and Excite. In addition, some sites have their own search engine to help you locate information within their site.

Netscape

Practice these steps to use a search engine. When you are ready to exit Netscape Navigator, see "Exiting Your Computer Session" on page 22.

If you are using Netscape Navigator, follow these steps to use a search engine:

1. Click on the Net Search directory button, and choose one of the search engines that appear on your screen.
   Note: Net Search allows you to link to numerous search engines; scroll to the end of this page to choose a search engine. You may also go directly to a particular search engine immediately after you launch your browser by typing the URL for the desired search engine in the Location box. For example, you can type **http://www.yahoo.com/** in the Location box and press ENTER/RETURN. Netscape Navigator will take you directly to the Yahoo home page.

2. In the search text box, type **white house**, and click on the Search button. Netscape Navigator will begin the searching process.
   Note: You may need to scroll down the page to locate the search text box.

The results of your search may include links to information all over the world.

3. Netscape Navigator will display the search results. Explore the links that interest you.
   Note: Be aware that searching at different times may bring different results. You can print a page by clicking on the Print button from your browser, or you can save a page by choosing *Save As* from the **File** menu.

4. When you find a page that you like, you can create a bookmark and let Netscape Navigator keep track of the URL. Go now to a web page that you like.

A bookmark flags the location of a document. You can create as many bookmarks as you want.

5. From the **Bookmarks** menu, choose *Add Bookmark*. You just marked this page for future use. Netscape Navigator will remember the URL and display the name of the document in your list of bookmarks.

6. You can easily access your bookmarks by choosing the **Bookmarks** menu. Then scroll through the list to find the page you want to visit. Within seconds, Netscape Navigator will link to the page.
   Note: To delete a bookmark, choose the *Go to Bookmark* option, highlight the bookmark in the list, and press DELETE.

7. Return to the Netscape Navigator home page.

Explorer

Practice these steps to use a search engine. When you are ready to exit Microsoft Internet Explorer, see "Exiting Your Computer Session" on page 22.

If you are using Microsoft Internet Explorer, follow these steps to use a search engine:

1. Click the Search button on the Toolbar.
   Note: The Search option allows you to link to numerous search engines from a single page. You may also go directly to a particular search engine immediately after you launch your browser by typing the URL for the desired search engine in the Address box. For example, you may type **http://www.yahoo.com/** in the Address box and press ENTER/RETURN. Internet Explorer will take you directly to the Yahoo home page.

The results of your search may include links to information all over the world.

2. In the search text box, type **white house**, and click on the Search button. Microsoft Internet Explorer will begin the searching process.

3. Your browser will display the search results. Explore the links that interest you.
   Note: Be aware that searching at different times may bring different results. You can print a page by clicking on the Print button from your browser, or you can save a page by choosing *Save As* from the **File** menu.

4. When you find a page that you like, you can create a bookmark and let Microsoft Internet Explorer keep track of the URL. Go now to a web page that you like.

A bookmark flags the location of a document. You can create as many bookmarks as you want.

5. From the **Favorites** menu, choose *Add to Favorites*. You just marked this page for future use. Microsoft Internet Explorer will remember the URL and display the name of the document in your list of favorites.

6. You can easily access your favorite pages by choosing the **Favorites** menu or by clicking the Favorites button. Then scroll through the list to find the page you want to visit. Within seconds, Microsoft Internet Explorer will link to the page.
   Note: To delete a bookmark, choose *Organize Favorites* from the **Favorites** menu. Highlight the bookmark you want to remove, and click the Delete button.

7. Return to the Microsoft Internet Explorer home page.

▶ ACCESSING GOPHER SITES

You can use your browser to access Gopher sites.

Gopher is a menu-based tool that allows you to search millions of directories and databases of text documents throughout the Internet. When you access gopher sites, you navigate from one menu to another menu and to submenus by choosing menu items until you find information that interests you. Gopher menus are usually very plain, with only hypertext links. If you find a menu or page that you may want to visit again, remember to add a bookmark. The URL for a gopher site begins with **gopher://**.

Netscape

If you are using Netscape Navigator, follow these steps to access gopher sites:

The URL for a gopher site begins with **gopher:**.

1. Go to the Library of Congress' Marvel gopher site at this URL: **gopher://marvel.loc.gov/**

2. Review the hypertext links on the gopher menu, and choose *Copyright*.
   Note: With gopher, you will dig through menus and more menus.

3. Another gopher menu will appear. Choose *Copyright Basics*. After digging through two menus, you now have a page on your screen to read.
   Note: Realize that searching at different times may bring different results; add a bookmark when you find a page you want to revisit. You can print a page by clicking on the Print button, or you can save a file by choosing *Save As* from the **File** menu.

4. Click on the Back button to review the menus and explore for other pages that interest you.

Explorer

If you are using Microsoft Internet Explorer, follow these steps to access gopher sites:

1. Go to the Library of Congress' Marvel gopher site at this URL:
   gopher://marvel.loc.gov/

2. Review the hypertext links on the gopher menu, and choose *Copyright*.
   Note: With gopher, you will dig through menus and more menus.

3. Another gopher menu will appear. Choose *Copyright Basics*. After digging through two menus, you now have a page on your screen to read.
   Note: Realize that searching at different times may bring different results; add a bookmark when you find a page you want to revisit. You can print a page by clicking on the Print button, or you can save a file by choosing *Save As* from the **File** menu.

4. Click on the Back button to review the menus and explore for other pages that interest you.

 RETRIEVING FTP FILES

One of the most popular uses of the Internet is the ability to **download** (or retrieve and copy) files from one computer to another. **File Transfer Protocol**, or FTP, was devised to retrieve a file that is on a computer located anywhere on the Internet. FTP files include freeware or shareware programs, publications, clip art, and many others.

FTP web pages are usually very plain, with only hypertext links and information about the files. For some FTP files, such as text documents, you can download the file and display it immediately on your screen. Other documents (for example, word processing, spreadsheet, or database) may have to be downloaded and then opened by running the appropriate program. For example, to open an Excel spreadsheet, you must have the Microsoft Excel software. For software programs, you must download such FTP files directly to a file on your hard drive. Then you may have to uncompress the file before you can run the program.

Netscape

If you are using Netscape Navigator, follow these steps to retrieve an FTP file:

1. Go to the Library of Congress FTP site at this URL:
   ftp://ftp.loc.gov/pub/

2. Notice the Folder (directory) and Document icons. Click on a directory icon to display a new list of files.
   Note: Notice the hypertext link Up to higher level directory at the beginning of the list. If you explored, click on this link to return to the */pub/* directory.

3. Link to the *README* file. A document called "Library of Congress Files Available through FTP" will appear on your screen.

4. From the **File** menu, choose *Save As*. Then verify the directory (folder) and drive where you want to save the file.

5. Type **ftpinfo** for the file name, and save the file to disk.

Explorer

If you are using Microsoft Internet Explorer, follow these steps to retrieve an FTP file:

1. Go to the Library of Congress FTP site at this URL:
    ftp://ftp.loc.gov/pub/

2. Click on a directory name to display a new list of files.
    Note: Notice the hypertext link <u>Up to higher level directory</u> at the beginning of the list. If you explored, click on this link to return to the */pub/* directory.

3. Link to the *README* file. A document called "Library of Congress Files Available through FTP" will appear on your screen.

4. From the **File** menu, choose *Save As*. Then verify the directory (folder) and drive where you want to save the file.

5. Type **ftpinfo** for the file name, and save the file to disk.

> **Before you download a program file to a school computer, ask permission from your teacher. Then to avoid contaminating your computer, always run a virus checker on the file.**

▶ COMMUNICATING WITH OTHERS

You can communicate with others who are connected to the Internet through e-mail communications, mailing lists, and news and conference areas. Because no one governs the Internet in terms of behavior and ethics, you should practice basic **netiquette**, or network etiquette, in all your e-mail communications. Consider these basic netiquette guidelines:

> **Practice basic netiquette in all your communications.**

- Always use a subject line in each e-mail message. This will allow the receiver to glance quickly at the e-mail message and have an idea of the topic of the message.

- Limit each e-mail message to one subject.

- Write clear, concise messages.

- Use upper- and lowercase letters in your messages.

- Use correct spelling, grammar, and punctuation.

- Use emoticons with caution. As shown in the following examples, an **emoticon** is a combination of symbols and letters that when combined display a little picture that expresses an emotion when you tilt your head to the left side.

  | :-) | smiling | ;-o | Oh My! |
  | ;-} | laughing while winking | : - (| sad |

- Use abbreviations as appropriate. Here are a few common abbreviations:

BTW	by the way
BRB	be right back
GMTA	great minds think alike
FYI	for your information

- Watch the tone of your message. Your word choice and how you explain things will determine the tone of your message.

- Always include your name (or signature) at the end of each message.

- Always communicate in a responsible manner. Realize that the receiver may share your message with others. And also realize that once you send your message, you cannot take it back.

> **Be responsible for understanding and following your school's computer use policy.**

Using Your E-Mail Software

Technically known as **electronic mail**, e-mail is the transfer of information in electronic format. With e-mail you will be able to send messages to and receive messages from anyone in the world who has an e-mail address whenever you want. As shown in Figure 1-6, an e-mail message has a heading, body, and signature.

Figure 1-6
Message Composition Window with Netscape Navigator Mail

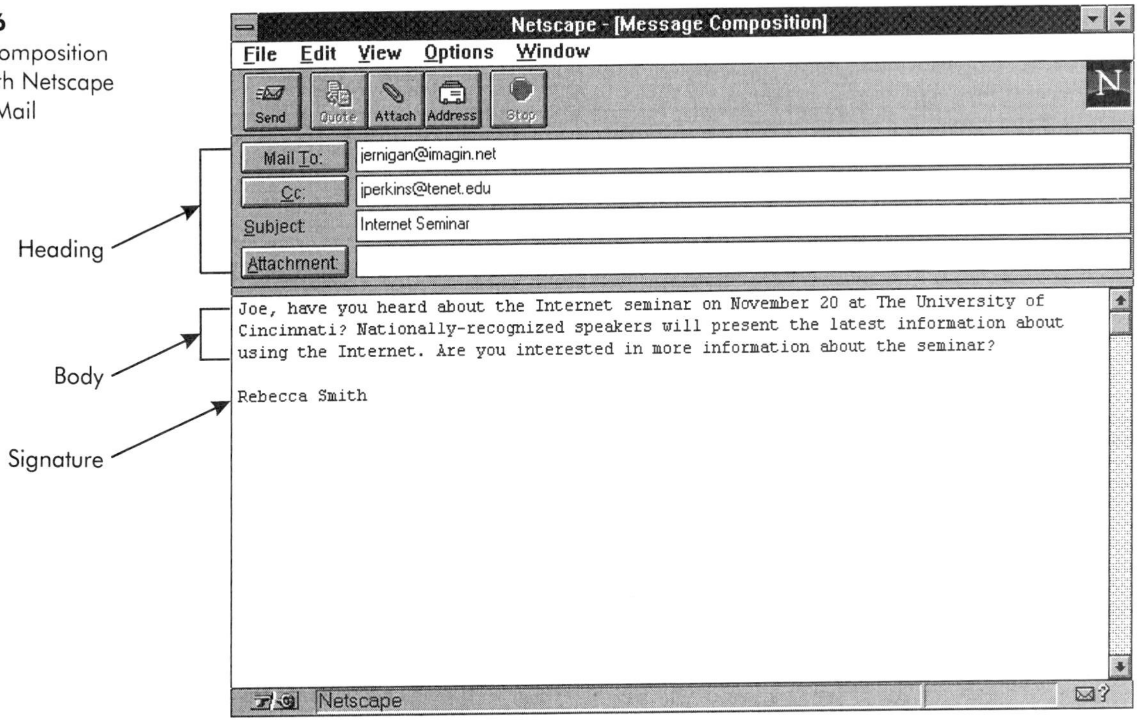

Heading

Body

Signature

Before you use your e-mail software, access online help to read about the features of your software.

Telecommunications systems use different tools to manage e-mail and to communicate on the Internet. These tools, often called **e-mail managers** or **mail readers**, may be built into the communications software you are using. Your e-mail manager will allow you to compose, read, print, save, and delete mail messages.

Netscape

If you are using Netscape Navigator, follow these steps to use your e-mail software:

1. Choose the e-mail option. You may have an envelope icon to click, or you may choose the *Netscape Mail* option in the **Window** menu.

Creating an E-Mail Message

2. Let's assume you want to send an e-mail message to one of your teachers about your study of e-mail and the Internet. Choose the option to create a new mail message. The message composition window will open. *Note:* You may have to type a password to have access to your e-mail software. If so, your teacher will tell you the password.

3. In the *To:* field, type the teacher's Internet address. Your teacher will provide the address to use.

4. Do not type anything in the *Cc:* field.
   Note: You would type an Internet address in this area only when you want to send a copy of your message to someone at the same time that you send the original message.

5. Move to the *Subject:* field, and type **Learning E-Mail**.
   Note: To move from one field to another, use the TAB key.

6. Do not type anything in the *Attachment:* field. You would type in this area only when you want to send files as attachments to a mail message.

Remember to follow the rules of netiquette.

7. Move to the message field, and type this message:

   [*Insert teacher's name*]**, you will be pleased to know that I am learning to use e-mail and the Internet. I'll soon be able to communicate with people all over the world. When I learn to use the Internet, I'll have many opportunities for hours of adventure, education, and fun.**

   [*Insert your name*]

8. Always proofread and edit your message to correct grammar, punctuation, and spelling errors.

9. Now that you have composed and edited your message, you are ready to send the message. Click on the Send button. You have now sent your e-mail message into cyberspace!

Reading an E-Mail Message

10. Whenever you want to read mail messages that were sent to you, choose the option to get mail or to view mail. After a brief pause, you will see a list of the files in your inbox.

11. Click a folder to display its messages. Choose the message *Welcome to the Internet!*
    Note: Your teacher should have sent you a *Welcome to the Internet!* e-mail message.

12. Read the entire message. Use the scroll bar and ARROW keys to view the other pages of the message.

13. As you read the message, think about whether you will want to print, save, download, or delete the message.

Printing an E-Mail Message

14. To print the message you have open on your screen, click on the Print button.

Saving an E-Mail Message

15. To save the message you have open on your screen to a new folder, choose the option to create a new folder. Type the name of the folder. You'll see the name of the new folder appear in the listing of folders in the message heading pane.

16. In the message heading pane, drag the name of the file to the newly created folder.
    Note: If you want to save a message to an existing folder, drag the name of the file to the name of that folder.

Working with an E-Mail Message

17. If you want to work with your e-mail message in your word processor, you must save the message as a text file. From the list of messages in your inbox, choose the message you want to download.

18. Choose *Save As* from the **File** menu, type the file name, and save the file as text to disk.
    Note: You can also copy a message and paste it into a word processing document.

Deleting an E-Mail Message

19. If you want to delete a message, highlight the message in the list of messages, and click on the Delete button.

Closing the E-Mail Software

20. To return to your browser, close the e-mail window.

Explorer

If you are using Microsoft Internet Explorer, follow these steps to use your e-mail software:

1. Click on the Mail button.

Creating an E-Mail Message

2. Let's assume you want to send an e-mail message to one of your teachers about your study of e-mail and the Internet. Choose the option to create a new mail message. The message composition window will open.

3. In the *To:* field, type the teacher's Internet address. Your teacher will provide the address to use.

4. Do not type anything in the *Cc:* field.
    Note: You would type an Internet address in this area only when you want to send a copy of your message to someone at the same time that you send the original message.

5. Move to the *Subject:* field, and type **Learning E-Mail**.
    Note: To move from one field to another, use the TAB key.

Remember to follow the rules of netiquette.

6. Move to the message field, and type this message:

    [*Insert teacher's name*], **you will be pleased to know that I am learning to use e-mail and the Internet. I'll soon be able to communicate with people all over the world. When I learn to use the Internet, I'll have many opportunities for hours of adventure, education, and fun.**

    [*Insert your name*]

7. Always proofread and edit your message to correct grammar, punctuation, and spelling errors.

8. Now that you have composed and edited your message, you are ready to send the message. Click on the Send button. You have now sent your e-mail message into cyberspace!

Reading an E-Mail Message

9. Whenever you want to read mail messages that were sent to you, choose the option to get mail or to read mail. After a brief pause, you will see a list of the messages (if any) in your inbox.
   Note: You may have to click the Send and Receive button to download your mail.

10. Choose the message *Welcome to the Internet!*
    Note: Your teacher should have sent you a *Welcome to the Internet!* e-mail message.

11. Read the entire message. Use the scroll bar and ARROW keys to view the other pages of the message.

12. As you read the message, think about whether you will want to print, save, download, or delete the message.

Printing an E-Mail Message

13. To print the message you have open on your screen, click on the Print button.

Saving an E-Mail Message

14. To save the message you have open on your screen, choose the *Save As* option from the **File** menu. Type a file name and save the file to disk.

Working with an E-Mail Message

15. If you want to work with your e-mail message in your word processor, you can copy/paste the message or save it to disk as a text file.

16. Choose *Save As* from the **File** menu, type the file name, and select the option to save as text.

Deleting an E-Mail Message

17. If you want to delete a message, highlight the message in the list of messages, and click on the Delete button.

Closing the E-Mail Software

18. To return to your browser, close the e-mail window.

Joining a Mailing List or Listserv

If you have a special interest, you might want to subscribe to a mailing list or listserv. A **listserv** is a discussion group focused on a particular interest area. Each listserv is composed of people who have voluntarily subscribed themselves. When one member of the listserv posts a message to the listserv, all members of the listserv will receive an e-mail message in their mailbox.

Therefore, if you subscribe to a list, check your mail regularly. Because subscribing to a mailing list can generate a lot of mail, you will soon get to know others who share interests similar to your own.

Important: There is no charge for joining a listserv. Just make sure you have your teacher's permission before you join a listserv.

Thousands of mailing lists exist on the Internet. To find a listserv that interests you, read books that provide lists of listservs by topic area, use a search engine and appropriate keywords, talk with others, or request a global list of listservs with an e-mail message.
Note: If you request a global list of listservs, use this address: **listserv@listserv.net** in your e-mail message. Your message should be as follows: **lists global/topic**. Insert the topic that interests you. When you receive the list, study it carefully to find the listservs that interest you.

Netscape

If you are using Netscape Navigator, follow these steps to join a listserv:

1. Select the e-mail option.

2. Because you must send an e-mail message to subscribe to a listserv, choose the option to create a new mail message.

3. In the *To:* field, type **listserv@** followed by the administrative address for the listserv.
   Note: The administrative address will be the second line of the resource listing.

   Important: Before you complete these steps, ask your teacher for permission to subscribe to a listserv and the name of the listserv.

4. Do not type anything in these fields: *Cc:*, *Subject:*, and *Attachment:*.
   Note: You may receive a prompt asking whether you want to include a subject. You do not want to include one.

5. Move to the message field, and type **subscribe** *listname your name*
   Note: Replace *listname* with the name of the listserv in which you are interested. Replace *your name* with your name.

6. Click on the Send button.

7. After a brief pause you will receive a confirmation request from the listserv. Use the reply feature of your e-mail software, and type this message: **OK**. You have now subscribed to a listserv.
   Note: Remember to check your e-mail frequently. You may receive lots of mail.

8. If you want to unsubscribe to a listserv, repeat steps 1 through 6 except type this message: **unsubscribe** *listname*
   Note: Replace *listname* with the name of the listserv. Your address will be removed from the listserv.

Explorer

If you are using Microsoft Internet Explorer, follow these steps to join a listserv:

1. Select the e-mail option.

2. Because you must send an e-mail message to subscribe to a listserv, choose the option to create a new mail message.

3. In the *To:* field, type **listserv@** followed by the administrative address for the listserv.
Note: The administrative address will be the second line of the resource listing.

   Important: Before you complete these steps, ask your teacher for permission to subscribe to a listserv and the name of the listserv.

4. Do not type anything in these fields: *Cc* or *Subject.*
Note: You may receive a prompt asking whether you want to include a subject. You do not want to include one.

5. Move to the message field, and type **subscribe** *listname your name*
Note: Replace *listname* with the name of the listserv in which you are interested. Replace *your name* with your name.

6. Click on the Send button.

7. After a brief pause you will receive a confirmation request from the listserv. Use the reply feature of your e-mail software, and type this message: **OK.** You have now subscribed to a listserv.
Note: Remember to check your e-mail frequently. You may receive lots of mail.

8. If you want to unsubscribe to a listserv, repeat steps 1 through 6 except type this message: **unsubscribe** *listname*
Note: Replace *listname* with the name of the listserv. Your address will be removed from the listserv.

Accessing News and Conference Areas

The newsgroups to which you have access may depend on the service your ISP provides. Your teacher will tell you whether you have access to newsgroups.

Just like the newspaper that you may have delivered to your doorstep, news is delivered to your computer on a monthly, daily, hourly, and minute-by-minute basis on the Internet. Most news services update articles (or postings) as the news happens, and they organize the articles by topic. **Newsgroups** or **conferences** provide areas for you to exchange ideas, ask questions, offer opinions, or just do some **lurking** (reading without expressing an opinion to the group). Most news and conference areas are organized according to related topics. You can choose a topic to investigate and read specific news articles. If you want to communicate with others on the topic, you can reply to an article.

Netscape

If you are using Netscape Navigator, follow these steps to access a newsgroup:

Important: As you explore newsgroups, always remember to leave an objectionable site quickly by clicking the Home button. You will immediately return to the home page set up for your browser.

1. If you know the name of the newsgroup you want to access, type **news:** followed by the name in the Location box of the browser, and skip to step 6. For example, type **news:biz.general** and press ENTER/RETURN.

Newsgroup articles are plain text with limited links.

2. To find a newsgroup, choose *Netscape News* from the **Window** menu. To view the list of newsgroups offered by your ISP, open the news folder, and choose *Show All Newsgroups* from the **Options** menu. An

alphabetical list of newsgroups will appear. This process may take a few minutes the first time the newsgroup list is downloaded to your computer.

3. Scroll down to the *biz.❖* folder. This newsgroup is dedicated to business topics.

4. Open the folder to display a list of the various newsgroups.

5. Select the *biz.general* newsgroup. After a few moments a list of articles will appear.
   Note: You may use the Find option on the **File** menu to search for specific text in articles.

6. Choose an article that interests you.

7. Read the article when it appears on your screen.

8. After you read the article, you can mail, save, download, print, or react to the article. Access online help for the steps to perform these actions.
   Note: If you reply to the article, remember that everyone in the newsgroup will read your reply.

9. When you are finished reading articles from the newsgroup, close the newsgroup window.

Explorer

If you are using Microsoft Internet Explorer, follow these steps to access a newsgroup:

Important: As you explore newsgroups, always remember to leave an objectionable site quickly by clicking the Home button. You will immediately return to the home page set up for your browser.

1. If you know the name of the newsgroup you want to access, type **news:** followed by the name in the Address box of the browser, and skip to step 5. For example, type **news:biz.general** and press ENTER/RETURN.

Newsgroup articles are plain text with limited links.

2. To find a newsgroup, click the Mail button and choose *Read News*. To view the list of newsgroups offered by your ISP, click the *Newsgroups* button. An alphabetical list of newsgroups will appear. This process may take a few minutes the first time the newsgroup list is downloaded to your computer.

3. Type **biz** in the *Display newsgroups which contain:* field, and then scroll to the *biz.general* newsgroup. This newsgroup is dedicated to business topics.

4. Select the *biz.general* newsgroup, and click the Go to button. After a few moments a list of articles will appear.
   Note: Do not subscribe to any newsgroups if the program prompts you to do so.

5. Choose an article that interests you.

6. Read the article when it appears on your screen.

7. After you read the article, you can mail, save, download, print, or react to the article. Access online help for the steps to perform these actions.
   Note: If you reply to the article, remember that everyone in the newsgroup will read your reply.

8. When you are finished reading articles from the newsgroup, close the newsgroup window.

Exiting Your Computer Session

Just as you will learn how to surf the Net on a routine basis, you will quickly learn how to quit your session at the computer.

Netscape

If you are using Netscape Navigator, follow these steps to end your computer session:

1. Click on the **File** menu.

2. Choose *Exit* (Windows) or *Quit* (Macintosh).

Explorer

If you are using Microsoft Internet Explorer, follow these steps to end your computer session:

1. Click on the **File** menu.

2. Choose *Exit* (Windows) or *Quit* (Macintosh).

One Two Three

1 2 3

Activities

Activity 1
Choosing an Internet Service Provider

It seems that everyone these days is either "on the Net" or wants to learn more about it. What? You too? Great! You already know that you need a computer, modem, and browser software to connect to the World Wide Web. But what else is needed to get on the Internet? Don't forget the Internet service provider (ISP). Accessing the "information superhighway" is the primary purpose of an Internet service provider (sometimes called an Internet access provider). An ISP is your gateway to the Internet.

Selecting an Internet service provider is much like choosing which kind of car you wish to purchase. Like cars, most ISPs perform essentially the same functions but vary according to options and price. By shopping the market for an ISP, you can make an informed decision as to which one best fits your needs.

Some companies, such as America Online (AOL), CompuServe, and Prodigy, provide Internet access and a wide range of other special options. Many ISPs, however, provide only basic Internet access. Depending on the service you choose, the online charges may also vary. Some provide unlimited access for one flat monthly fee. Others charge a lower fee for a few hours of connect time per month, but they charge by the hour if you exceed a preset limit. By learning about the options available, you will be better prepared to select an Internet service provider that meets your needs.

After you complete this activity, you will be able to:

- Create a database to track Internet service provider information.
- Collect and store information about ISPs in a database.
- Define the terms related to Internet service providers.
- Compose a survey.
- Combine data from separate databases.
- Analyze cost data and other information to assist in choosing an ISP.
- Compose a report.

To collect and analyze data about Internet service providers, follow these steps:

Use the same database layout and field names to facilitate creating a combined database.

1. Using your database software, create a new database to track information about Internet service providers. The database should include at least the following information:

   ISP Name
   URL Address
   SLIP/PPP Monthly Fee
   Shell Account Monthly Fee
   Setup Charge
   Hourly Rate

   Personal Web Page Support
   Web Page Size Limit
   Web Page Cost
   Macintosh/Windows Support
   Other

Plan the layout of the database so that you can combine the data you collect individually with the databases from other students in your class.

2. Launch your browser software, and connect to the Internet.

3. A comprehensive list of Internet service providers is available at The List web site at this URL: **http://thelist.com/**
   Your screen should be similar to The List home page in Figure 2-1. Explore this web site to find Internet service providers in your area.

Search by area code to quickly find the ISPs in your area.

Figure 2-1
The List Home Page

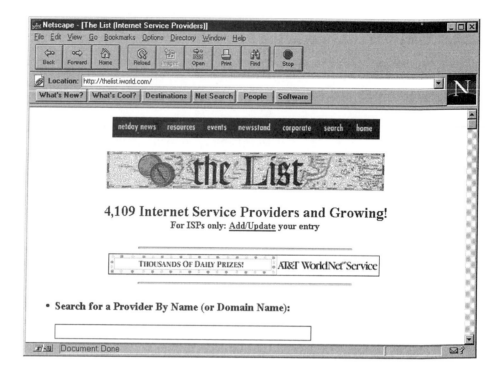

4. Select at least five local Internet service providers from the list.

   If other students in your class are working on this activity, decide which ISPs you should research to avoid duplications. When you finish this activity, you will combine the data you gathered with other teams' data to create a comprehensive database. Be sure to prioritize the tasks required to complete this activity by the deadline set by your teacher. *Note:* Be sure to gather data about your current ISP.

Use the Internet to learn more about any terms, acronyms, or topics you do not understand.

5. Link to the ISP sites to gather the information for your database. Remember that you can save the information shown on a page and refer to it later while you work off-line.

6. Use an Internet search engine to locate additional ISPs in your state that you have not already researched. You may want to choose a search engine from among the URLs listed below.

   AltaVista   **http://www.altavista.digital.com/**
   Lycos   **http://www.lycos.com/**
   Excite   **http://www.excite.com/**
   Magellan   **http://www.mckinley.com/**
   Yahoo   **http://www.yahoo.com/**

You may want to use **ISP** or **Internet service provider** as keywords along with your city and state to limit the scope of your search. Once you locate other ISPs, gather appropriate information to update your database.

7. Exit your browser software.

8. Using your database, record the information you collected. Be sure to enter the data in the appropriate fields.

9. Generate a report about the Internet service providers you researched. Carefully proof the data and make any corrections, if necessary.

Make a backup of your database before attempting to combine it with another database.

10. Working as a team, determine how to combine separate databases into one comprehensive database. Use the database software help and user's guide to learn more about this process. Verify with your teacher the steps required to join databases.

11. Perform the steps to join the individual databases into one database.

12. Arrange the data based on cost. Generate a report and analyze the data.

13. As a team, design and compose a brief survey to determine which service providers the businesses in your area use to connect to the Internet. Gather the information by letter, through e-mail, by telephone, or in person. Assign each team member to one or more local businesses.

   The survey should include questions such as:
   ▶ What ISP do you currently use?
   ▶ How long have you used this ISP?
   ▶ How much do you pay per month?
   ▶ What factors were important to you in choosing your Internet service provider?

14. Conduct the survey and compile the results.

15. Using your word processing software, compose a report to summarize your findings. Use the information you gathered about the local ISPs and the results of your survey to prepare the report.
   ▶ Which ISP is the least expensive?
   ▶ What other factors are important to consider when choosing an ISP?
   ▶ Which ISPs do businesses in your area use?
   ▶ What factors did they use in making their selection?

Activity 2
Using Citation and Copyright Resources

The Internet, as you already know, provides access to vast information resources. With a computer and modem you can quickly find information that once required hours and even days to locate. Search engines make this process even easier by placing the entire Internet at your fingertips.

Before the World Wide Web, you probably relied on encyclopedias and other reference books to perform your research. Although this new technology allows you to work more efficiently, the same citation and copyright guidelines apply to this new research tool as to print materials. Always remember to acknowledge those resources that were helpful by citing electronic resources properly. And you should fully understand the copyright issues, since technology makes copying information so easy. Resources are available online that explain the proper formatting guidelines for citations. Other resources provide information on the copyright laws.

After you complete this activity, you will be able to:

- Research citation and copyright resources information.
- Explain how to cite both electronic and print resources in a research paper.
- Discuss the proper use of copyrighted information.
- Prepare a research paper using the appropriate citation and style guidelines.
- Present your findings.

To learn about citation and copyright resources, follow these steps:

1. Select a topic for a research project. Choose from among the following topics; or if you were assigned a research topic in another class, you may be able to use that topic.
   Note: Discuss your topic with your teacher before proceeding.
   History and Development of the Internet
   Growth of Intranets as the Means for Businesses to Communicate with Employees
   Use of the Internet to Deliver Educational Content
   Impact of Technological Change on Information Systems Professionals
   Information Systems Careers
   Social and Ethical Impact of Technology

2. Launch your browser software, and connect to the Internet.

3. Link to the Citation and Copyright Resources web site at this URL:
   http://www.tenet.edu/library/citation.html
   Review the resources that discuss how to cite electronic resources. As shown in Figure 2-2 on page 29, you can explore numerous resources on

Remember that you can save web pages and review them later while working off-line.

Figure 2-2
TENET Citation and Copyright Resources Web Page

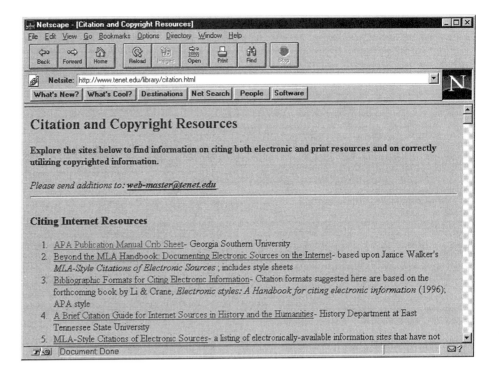

this page. As you explore the information, note any differences in the recommended styles and formats.

Although you can expand your search, be sure to at least explore these resources:

APA Publication Manual Crib Sheet
Beyond the MLA Handbook: Documenting Electronic Sources on the Internet
Bibliographic Formats for Citing Electronic Information
A Brief Citation Guide for Internet Sources in History and the Humanities
MLA-Style Citations of Electronic Sources
Using APA Format—Purdue University Writing Lab

4. Go back to the Citations and Copyright Resources page. Review the frequently asked questions (FAQs) concerning copyright issues. Consider the following questions as you prepare to write a research paper.

▸ What is a copyright?
▸ What are the guidelines for including information in a research paper?
▸ What is fair use?
▸ What precautions should you take to avoid copyright infringement?

5. Exit your browser software.

6. Using your word processing software, briefly summarize how to properly cite electronic resources. Provide examples where appropriate.

7. Discuss with your class and teacher the format to use for citations in your research paper. Also, discuss the copyright issues about which you learned.

Next time you are online, link to the resource that matches your teacher's standards, and set a bookmark. Refer to this location as you research the topic you selected.

Refer to the online help provided by the search engines to help you locate relevant information.

Always ask your teacher for permission before you subscribe to a newsgroup.

8. Begin your research project. Launch your browser software, as needed, to find information online. Use any of these search engines to locate web sites that pertain to your topic:

AltaVista	**http://www.altavista.digital.com/**
Lycos	**http://www.lycos.com/**
Excite	**http://www.excite.com/**
Magellan	**http://www.mckinley.com/**
Yahoo	**http://www.yahoo.com/**

9. Extend your online research to include newsgroups, if appropriate. Simply read those articles available on your topic, or start your own discussion.

10. Organize your research notes, and then use your word processing or desktop publishing software to prepare your report. Be sure to support your research with charts, graphs, and other data. Remember to include the appropriate citations.

11. Prepare an oral presentation of your research findings. Using your presentation software, prepare related visual aids for the oral presentation.

Activity 3
Exploring Ethics and the Internet

As with any new technology such as the Internet, potential for misuse exists. Confidentiality, lack of privacy, and security issues are among the many concerns that anyone who uses the Internet must understand. Are e-mail messages confidential? Can you buy merchandise online using a credit card without worrying about someone illegally obtaining this information? Can anyone access the information on your computer?

Although the media tends to exaggerate these concerns, unethical use of technology is an issue that everyone should take seriously. Everyone needs to be aware of the consequences that occur as a result of unethical practices. You not only need to know how to protect yourself against any unethical computer use but also how to use technology and the Internet responsibly.

Many web sites on the Internet focus on ethical issues pertaining to computers and technology. These sites provide up-to-date information on ethical concerns that affect all of us. Other resources present common sense guidelines that are relevant to anyone who uses a computer at work, at home, or at school.

After you complete this activity, you will be able to:

- Search for web sites that discuss ethics and the Internet.
- Use the Internet responsibly.
- Search for newsgroups that discuss computer ethics.
- Explain appropriate ethical practices and expectations as an Internet user.
- Prepare a report.

To learn more about ethics and the Internet, follow these steps:

1. Launch your browser software, and connect to the Internet.

2. Many resources on the World Wide Web are devoted to ethics. One of these is provided by the School of Communications at California State University, Fullerton. Link to their web site at this URL:
   http://www5.fullerton.edu/les/ethics_list.html
   Your screen should be similar to the page in Figure 2-3 on page 32.

   > **This site includes *www5* as part of the domain name. Network administrators sometimes include a digit as part of the name when there are multiple servers at a location.**

3. Link to Computer Ethics.

   This web page provides links to several resources that focus on computer ethics. (See Figure 2-4 on page 32.) For example, you can access the Computer Ethics Institute web page from here. Other Internet resources include NetEthics Committee of the Computer Law Section of the State Bar of Georgia, UC Berkeley, and the British Government.

   > **Be sure to link to the Ten Commandments of Computer Ethics on the Computer Ethics Institute web site.**

4. Explore the links to the web sites that discuss computer ethics. Review at least five articles on this subject. Gather information to prepare a report on how to use the Internet responsibly. Save the information to review later off-line. Consider these questions:

Figure 2-3
California State University, Fullerton Web Site: Ethics on the World Wide Web

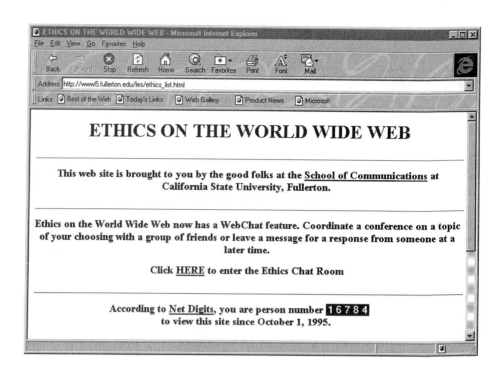

Figure 2-4
Computer Ethics Web Page

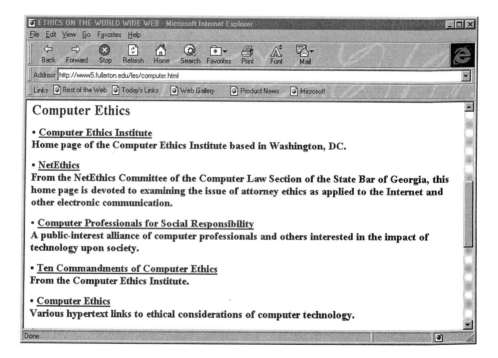

▶ What ethical issues are the most prevalent?

▶ List several significant ethical issues related to the use of computers.

▶ Do any of these issues affect you or someone you know?

▶ How can you responsibly use the Internet?

▶ Are the ethical issues about which you learned limited to your use of the computer in this class, or do they apply to the use of technology in other courses such as English, history, and science? How?

▶ What are the consequences of a breach of confidential information?

5. Use an Internet search engine to locate additional resources related to computer ethics.

6. Search the newsgroups to find any discussions on computer ethics.

7. The Ethics on the World Wide Web page contains a link to discuss ethics topics online. The "chat room" is similar to a newsgroup, but it is accessed only through this web page. Every time you post a message it appears on the page for everyone else in the chat room to see.

   Go back to the Ethics on the World Wide Web page at this URL:
   http://www5.fullerton.edu/les/ethics_list.html
   Link to the chat room. You can review the comments already posted or join in the discussion.

8. Go back to the Ethics on the World Wide Web page, and review the other topics. Choose at least one of the following areas to explore:

   Business Ethics
   Legal Ethics
   Media Ethics
   Science Ethics
   Medical Ethics
   Governmental Ethics

   ▶ Are there similar concerns between computer ethics and other areas?

   ▶ What ethical issues are unique to computers?

9. Exit your browser software.

10. Review the information you gathered during your research of this topic.

11. Using your word processing or desktop publishing software, prepare a report that describes your findings regarding computer ethics.

Activity 4
Analyzing Statistical Data

Today's youth are under tremendous pressure—school, work, family, and peer relationships. Statistical data gathered from several studies present insightful information that can help us understand these problems and address some possible solutions.

The National Center for Education Statistics web site offers access to many of the agency's publications, including one entitled *Youth Indicators 1996*. This publication provides a statistical compilation of data on family structure, jobs, education, and other elements that comprise the world of young people. The data also focuses on the home environment including demographics, family composition, and family income; the school environment including school descriptions, outcomes, and out-of-school experiences; health; citizenship and values; and students' futures.

Everyone can make a difference in tomorrow's world. If you analyze and understand the statistics, you can learn about the areas that need improvement and leverage this knowledge to facilitate change. For example, tobacco, alcohol, and drug use represent a significant health risk to teens. Statistical data clearly identifies the risks involved, but the data also indicates that the problem is growing. By using data available on the Internet, you can inform others about these risks and take a proactive role in changing this trend.

After you complete this activity, you will be able to:

- Download statistical data.
- Download a software program.
- Analyze and interpret data presented in tables and charts.
- Create a bar or line chart to depict statistical data.
- Develop a plan of action to effect positive changes related to tobacco, alcohol, and drug use.
- Compose a letter to describe your plan of action.

To analyze and interpret statistical data, follow these steps:

1. Launch your browser software, and connect to the Internet.

2. The National Center for Education Statistics (NCES) publishes information on its web page that shows the condition and progress of education in the United States and other nations. The purpose of this organization is to help improve American education. The agency offers many publications including those that focus on pertinent youth indicators.

   Access the National Center for Education Statistics (NCES) web site at this URL: **http://www.ed.gov/NCES/**

   Your screen should be similar to the National Center for Education Statistics (NCES) web page in Figure 2-5 on page 35.

Remember, the contents and links on a web page may change at any time. When you explore a page looking for information, try to find links that match your search criteria.

Figure 2-5

National Center for Education Statistics Home Page

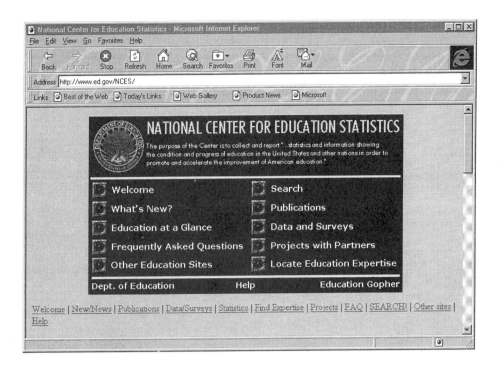

Use the search option provided at the NCES web site. Try **tobacco alcohol drug use** as the keywords.

3. Locate the most recent *Youth Indicators* publication. Then find the tobacco, alcohol, and drug use statistics. Save or print the information. Figure 2-6 shows a table that summarizes the findings presented in the 1996 report.

4. Link to the chart that shows the trends in tobacco, alcohol, and drug use since 1975. Save or print the chart to review later.

Figure 2-6

Youth Indicators 1996: Tobacco, Alcohol, and Drug Use Summary

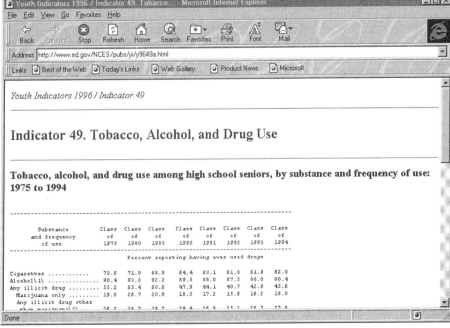

The acronym PDF is an abbreviation for portable document format.

5. *Optional:* Download the entire *Youth Indicators* publication as a single PDF file. You must have the Adobe Acrobat® Reader software to view this file. If you do not have access to the Acrobat Reader, you can download it free of charge from Adobe at this URL: http://www.adobe.com/

   Important: Check with your teacher to make sure that you should download the Acrobat Reader program to your computer from Adobe's web site. The download process may take 15–30 minutes or longer, depending on the speed of your Internet connection.

   Follow the steps given at the Adobe site to download the appropriate version of the Acrobat Reader for your system. You must choose from among several operating systems (Windows, Macintosh, OS/2, UNIX, and so on) and languages (English, French, German, and so on). Once you download the program, you may have to complete the process by running the program to install the software on your computer.

6. Exit your browser software.

7. Analyze the data and the chart that you downloaded from the National Center for Education Statistics page. Compare and contrast the changes over the years.

   ▶ Do you see a relationship between the data over the years?
   ▶ Does the data show increases or decreases?
   ▶ Are the increases or decreases steady or drastic from one year to the next?
   ▶ Is there a relationship between the different age groups?

Access online help to determine whether a bar or line chart will best depict your data.

8. Using your spreadsheet software, create a bar or line chart that shows a more detailed view of the statistical data you gathered.

9. Using your word processing or desktop publishing software, compose a report about your findings. Take a proactive approach and recommend alternative solutions in an action plan that will help reduce tobacco, drug, and alcohol use among teens. Be sure to support your recommendations with statistics.

Remember to proofread your report carefully for grammar, spelling, and punctuation errors.

10. Share your report with a classmate and a family member, asking for constructive criticism. Revise your plan as appropriate.

11. Compose and send a letter to your school administrators describing your plan of action. Ask permission to present the plan to the faculty, staff members, and your classmates. Be sure to include relevant statistical data to support your findings. Using your presentation software, prepare a visual aid for your presentation.

Activity 5
Learning About Youth Leadership Organizations

The Internet provides an opportunity for you to explore national youth business organizations. Two such organizations are Business Professionals of America (BPA) and Future Business Leaders of America (FBLA). Educators and business leaders acknowledge the benefits these organizations offer their members. Participation in either group helps prepare you for a leadership role in almost any business-related career.

Business Professionals of America and Future Business Leaders of America each have their own web site for you to learn more about the goals and activities of their organization. To foster leadership development among students, both organizations sponsor competitive events.

After you complete this activity, you will be able to:

- Identify the goals and activities of Business Professionals of America.
- Identify the purpose of Future Business Leaders of America.
- Compose an informative report about your findings.
- Prepare a poster to promote an upcoming event.
- Communicate with members of these organizations.

To learn more about youth business leadership organizations, follow these steps:

1. Find out whether your school sponsors a local chapter of either Business Professionals of America or Future Business Leaders of America. Answer the following questions if you have a chapter of these organizations at your school. If you do not, skip to step 2.
   Note: You may ask your teacher, a school administrator, or a classmate for the information.
   - Which organization does your school sponsor?
   - How many students participate in the organization?
   - Who is the sponsoring teacher for the organization?
   - When are the meetings for the organization?

2. Launch your browser software, and connect to the Internet.

3. Go to the Business Professionals of America web site at this URL:
   http://www.bpa.org/bpa.html
   Your screen should be similar to the Business Professionals of America home page in Figure 2-7 on page 38. From this page you can link to information about meetings and conferences, whom to contact, and chapter enrollment.

Scroll through information to locate the hypertext links you want to explore.

4. Explore the Business Professionals of America web site.
   - What are the goals of the organization?
   - Why was it formed?

Figure 2-7

Business Professionals of America Home Page

▶ Which companies have a partnership with Business Professionals of America? What assistance do these companies offer?

▶ In what ways can Business Professionals of America help you to improve your leadership skills?

▶ What events has Business Professionals of America sponsored within the past few months?

▶ What are the upcoming events?

▶ Do any upcoming events interest you?

5. If your school does not already have a Business Professionals of America chapter, investigate the requirements to begin a chapter.
Note: You may want to save or print the information.

▶ What are the membership requirements?

▶ Do any other chapters exist near your school?

6. Go to the Future Business Leaders of America web site at this URL: **http://www.fbla-pbl.org**
Your screen should be similar to the Future Business Leaders of America home page in Figure 2-8 on page 39. The Future Business Leaders of America web site helps to keep members up-to-date on the activities of the organization. The web site also provides an opportunity to disseminate information to prospective members.

7. Explore the Future Business Leaders of America web site.

▶ What are the goals and mission of the organization?

▶ What is the difference between Business Professionals of America and Future Business Leaders of America?

▶ How does Future Business Leaders of America attract members?

8. If your school does not have a local Future Business Leaders of America chapter, find the information needed to begin a chapter.
Note: You may want to save or print the information.

Figure 2-8
Future Business Leaders of
America Home Page

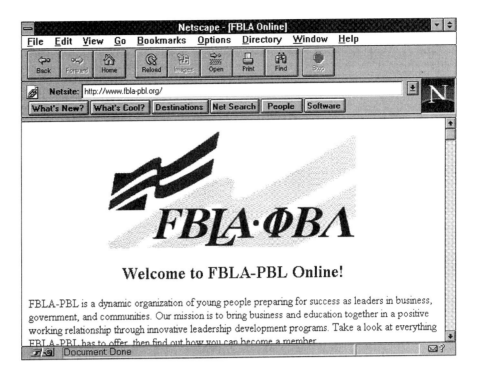

9. Exit your browser software.

10. Using your word processing software, compose an informative report to your teacher to present your findings.

Remember to proofread your report carefully to verify all grammar, punctuation, and spelling. Also include citations to give credit to others' material.

11. If you are a member of either organization, use a paint program or an illustration program to prepare a poster to promote an upcoming event or to share information with your school about something the organization is sponsoring (such as a contest or a scholarship). If your school has a chapter of Future Business Leaders of America or Business Professionals of America, secure information from a member about an upcoming event in order to prepare a poster. If your school does not have a chapter of Future Business Leaders of America or Business Professionals of America, prepare a poster for another school organization. *Note:* Copy the logo from the web page of your organization to use in the poster.

Access online help for the steps to copy an image on a web page.

   ▶ Identify the event.
   ▶ Identify the essential information about the event, such as the date, time, place, and so on.
   ▶ List the requirements to qualify for the event.
   ▶ Add borders or art to make the poster more attractive.

12. Now that you know more about Business Professionals of America and Future Business Leaders of America, communicate with members of these organizations if you are interested in joining either organization (if your school has a chapter). If your school does not have a local chapter of these organizations, communicate with your business teacher about starting one. In a team discussion, prepare a list of the benefits to students and the school of having a chapter at your school.

Activity 6
Funding Your College Education

Over a lifetime, a college-educated person will earn on average nearly $1 million more than a high school graduate. Earning a college degree, therefore, has a financial benefit as well as a strong educational value.

You must consider many factors when you decide which college to attend. One of the factors relates to how you will fund your college education. The average tuition, room, and board for a public university cost about $9,000 per year in 1996. Private schools cost much more—many over $20,000 per year. And costs continue to increase by about 8–10 percent per year.

How can you afford a college education? What options do you have? You could apply for an educational loan, secure part-time work to offset some of the expenses, or apply for a scholarship or grant. Knowing your options about funding your college education is the first step in the process. To learn more about student loans, scholarships, and grants, explore the Internet.

After you complete this activity, you will be able to:

- Locate college funding resources for student loans, scholarships, and grants.
- Identify the four basic types of financial aid.
- Use an online tool to help you plan your college education funding requirements.
- Explain student loan deferment and consolidation options.
- Create a database to track college funding options.
- Create a database report.
- Present your database.

To learn more about funding your college education, follow these steps:

1. Launch your browser software, and connect to the Internet.

2. Go to the College Funding Company web site at this URL:
   http://www.collegefundingco.org/
   Your screen should be similar to the College Funding Company web site in Figure 2-9 on page 41. This site publishes information about college education expenses and how to fund them. By exploring the College Funding Company web site, you can learn or review college funding information, begin the planning process, explore financial aid options, and estimate your college savings requirements.

3. Explore the web site to learn more about the types of financial aid.
   ▶ What are the four basic types of financial aid?
   ▶ Do you qualify for any of these?

Figure 2-9
College Funding
Company Home Page

4. Determine the availability of educational loans. Record the following information about each loan so that you can create a database with educational loan information after you explore the Internet.

   Loan
   Interest Rate
   Repayment
   Fees
   Limit

Look for the FAFSA link on the Financial Aid page.

5. Locate information on FAFSA.
   ▶ What is FASFA?
   ▶ How often do you need to apply?
   ▶ When is the best time to apply?
   ▶ What is the purpose of the application?

6. Locate information at the College Funding Company web site that explains loan repayment options if you were to get a student loan. This location should include a sample loan repayment schedule, loan deferment options, and loan consolidation information. You may also want to view a sample repayment schedule similar to the web page in Figure 2-10 on page 42.

   Gather information about deferment options and loan consolidation.
   ▶ Which loans do not begin to accrue interest during a deferment period?
   ▶ Which loan is the most commonly used student loan program?
   ▶ What are the three most common reasons for granting a loan deferment?
   ▶ What does it mean to "consolidate" your loans?

Figure 2-10
Sample Repayment
Schedule

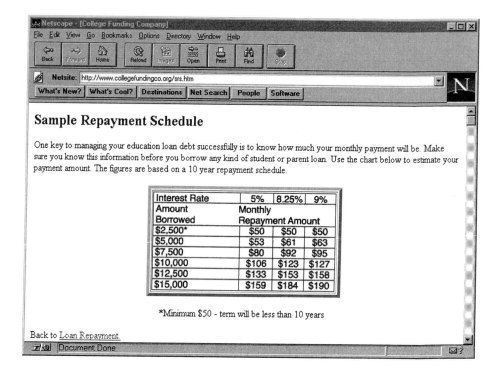

> ▶ What are the benefits of loan consolidation?
> ▶ What are the drawbacks of loan consolidation?

Try the Calculator link to locate the College Funding Planner. As you use the planner, you may want to link to one or more college web sites to find information on education costs.

7. Use the College Funding Planner to estimate the college costs you can expect in the future and how much money you must save toward these costs. Experiment with the planner to estimate different levels. For example, compare the cost to attend a public university with the cost to attend a private college.

> ▶ How much should you save per month to pay for college?
> ▶ What is the total investment?
> ▶ How much of the investment will you need to finance?

8. Explore the College Funding Estimator to learn the types of information you will need to provide. This tool can help you determine the amount of financial aid for which you qualify.
   Note: To complete the form, you must have information from your parents' income tax return. You may want to inform your parents about this tool.

9. Go to the Federal Information Exchange, Inc. web site at this URL:
   http://www.fie.com
   Explore the information at the Federal Information Exchange, Inc. site. As shown in Figure 2-11 on page 43, numerous options are provided at this web site that link higher education and the government.

> ▶ What is MOLIS?
> ▶ What scholarships or fellowships are available?
> ▶ Explain the purpose of FEDIX.

Figure 2-11
Federal Information
Exchange, Inc. Home Page

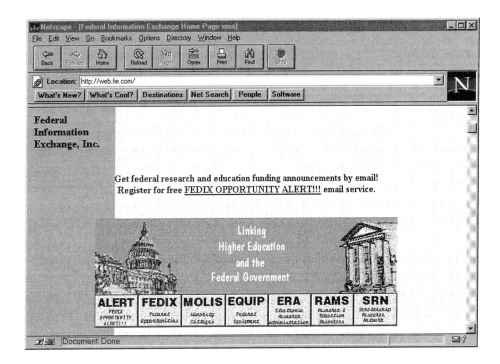

10. Link to the <u>Scholarship Resource Network</u>. Search for any available scholarships or loans. Record any information that you can include in your database on educational loans.

11. Continue your search for college funding information by using one of the commercial search engines. For example, go to the Yahoo web site, link to <u>Education</u> and then to <u>Financial Aid</u> for a list of potential resources.
    Note: You may want to save to disk or print the college funding information you discover.

12. Exit your browser software.

13. With your assigned team members, use your database software to plan the layout of a database for educational loan information. Decide whether to create one database for your entire class for the information on student loans, scholarships, and grants or whether to design separate databases.

14. Enter the data you collected in this activity into the database(s). Then create a database report that lists the information you gathered.

15. With your assigned team members, present your database to the class. Use an illustration program to prepare at least one visual aid. Generate a discussion on how you will use this information for lifelong learning purposes.

Activity 7
Preparing for a Job Interview

Someday you want to secure a rewarding job, don't you? To find the "perfect" job, you must thoroughly prepare yourself for the employment process. The employment process involves these stages:

- Planning for a career, which means assessing your strengths, skills, and personality; studying a career; setting goals; and making decisions to reach your goals.
- Preparing a résumé.
- Developing a cover letter to accompany your résumé.
- Preparing for a job interview.
- Developing other employment-related messages, such as a thank-you letter for an interview, an acceptance letter to accept a job offer, and a refusal letter to turn down a job offer.

In other activities you have focused on career planning and preparing a résumé. Your objective for sending a résumé and a cover letter to a prospective employer is to get an interview. After an employer arranges an interview, you must prepare for it. You don't want to assume your GPA or personality will persuade the prospective employer to hire you.

What is the purpose of an interview? An **interview** is an opportunity for a prospective employer to learn whether you would make a good "fit" for the company's needs. The first impression you make during the interview may be your only opportunity to persuade the employer that you are the right person for the position.

In today's world most people are likely to change jobs several times during their lifetimes. As a result you may expect to have several employment interviews to secure various positions. To improve your chances of receiving a job offer, you must learn how to prepare for an interview and how to develop your interviewing skills.

After you complete this activity, you will be able to:

- Assess your current knowledge of interviewing by participating in an interactive mock interview.
- Research interviewing tips from different web sites.
- Identify "do's" and "don'ts" of interviewing.
- Find a realistic position for which you could apply.
- Develop a résumé.
- Develop a letter of application.
- Conduct role-playing scenarios for realistic positions.
- Evaluate your own and each others' interviewing skills.
- Prepare a manual on interviewing.

To learn more about preparing for a job interview, follow these steps:

1. Launch your browser software, and connect to the Internet.

2. Go to the Kaplan's Career Center web site at this URL:
   http://www.kaplan.com/career/
   This site has an interactive game that allows you to assume the role of an interviewee. You read interview questions and respond appropriately based on your knowledge of interviewing.

   ▸ How would you rate your interviewing skills?

3. Let's see how your interviewing skills are by participating in the interactive mock interview. Link first to <u>The Hot Seat</u>. Read the information on this page and play the game.
   Note: In this interviewing game you will be asked common interviewing questions. Thoughtfully answer each interview question with your best response, and then submit each response. If, after any response, you receive a notice that your answers are not secured, select the continue button to proceed with the interview questions. If you receive a prompt to back up and select another answer, use your browser software to go back to the previous question.

4. Review the interpretation of your score and evaluate your interviewing skills.

   ▸ What is your score?
   ▸ How would you rate your interviewing skills now?
   ▸ What did you learn from playing this interactive game?

Save to disk or print information and images that you may want to include in your manual. Be sure to also record appropriate information for citations.

5. Go back to Kaplan's <u>Career Center</u>, and explore for information on interviews.

   ▸ What is an interview?
   ▸ Identify at least five tips you should consider to prepare for an interview.
   ▸ How can you get information about the company with which you have an interview?
   ▸ How can you prepare for the questions an employer might ask you during an interview?
   ▸ List at least five common interview questions.
   ▸ What should you do to follow up an interview?

6. Print the list of common questions asked during an interview. You'll need these questions later in this activity.

Scroll down through web pages to locate hypertext links that relate to interviewing.

7. Explore for information on interviewing at the web sites at these URLs: (See Figure 2-12 on page 46.)
   "Flatley Interview Checklist" at **http://www.flatley.com/check.htm**
   "Interview Tips" at **http://www.bc.edu/bc_org/svp/carct/ INTERVIEW.html**
   "The Art of the Interview" at **http://www.kiwicare.com/kiwi17.htm**
   "A Polished Interview" at **http://www.kiwicare.com/kiwi40.htm**
   "Job Interviews: Employer's Favorite Interview Questions" at **http://www.kiwicare.com/interview.htm**
   "Job Interviews: What Job Candidates Are Asking Employers" at **http://www.kiwicare.com/interview2.htm**

Figure 2-12
The Art of the Interview
Web Page

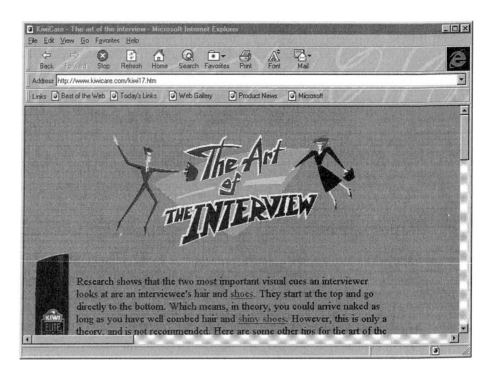

> Identify the basic styles of employment interviews.
> How should you prepare for an interview?
> What additional information did you learn that relates to the actual interview?
> What questions are illegal for an employer to ask?
> How do you handle illegal questions?
> What questions might you ask an employer during the interview?
> Identify several difficult questions that you might expect to be asked.
> Identify reasons why potential employees are rejected.
> How important is your attire for an interview?
> What factors influence an employer's impression of you during an interview?
> How important is a follow-up letter?
> Identify five major considerations in the negotiation process.

8. *Optional:* Search for a newsgroup that relates to employment practices. Explore related articles.
   Note: To find a newsgroup, you may want to go to the Deja News Research Service web site at **http://www.dejanews.com/**
   This site is a tool for searching through postings in thousands of newsgroups.
   Note: Be sure to record notes in your journal. You may also want to save to disk or print related information.

9. Using a search engine, conduct a search for additional information related to job interview skills.

10. Using a search engine, locate information about a position for which you could apply. You may want to narrow your search for positions to

The Deja News Research Service web site is free and easy to use.

your local community. Secure information about the company. You may also want to see whether any newsgroups identify relevant positions. *Note:* See whether the company has a web site. Then see if an e-mail address is given for you to request additional company information.

11. Exit your browser software.

> **A résumé is a one- or two-page summary that identifies your strengths, education, experience, and skills.**

12. Do you have a current résumé? Using your word processing software, develop a résumé that you could use to apply for the position you located. Exchange résumés with a classmate and offer constructive criticism to improve the appearance and the content of your résumé. *Note:* You may want to search the Internet for information related to developing a résumé or to view sample résumés. One site you may want to visit is The Purdue University On-line Writing Lab at **http://owl.trc.purdue.edu/**

   Remember to include all the critical information in your résumé to best represent who you are and what you have to offer a company.

> **A letter of application introduces yourself to a prospective employer and accompanies your résumé.**

13. Do you have a letter of application? Using your word processing software, develop a letter of application that you could send to accompany your résumé (assuming you were applying for the position you located). Exchange letters with a classmate and offer constructive criticism to improve the appearance and the content of your letter of application.
   Note: You may want to search the Internet for information related to developing a letter of application or to view sample letters. One site you may want to visit is The Purdue University On-line Writing Lab at **http://owl.trc.purdue.edu/**

14. In your assigned team, brainstorm to prepare a list of questions you might ask during an interview for your selected position.
   Note: Discuss the types of questions you have been asked in actual interviews for various types of jobs.

15. Let's apply your knowledge of interviewing to a role-playing situation. Your teacher will divide the class into teams for this step. Within your team one person will assume the role of the interviewee for the specific position he or she found on the Internet. The remaining team members will take turns being the interviewer. The interviewer should ask the interviewee common questions (see step 6 on page 45). Repeat this activity until each person in your team has assumed the role of an interviewee.
   Note: Critique each interviewee's performance. Consider these questions in your evaluation:

   ▶ How did each person handle the difficult questions?
   ▶ How would you rate each person's nonverbal communication?
   ▶ Would you hire the person for the job? Why or why not?
   ▶ Which team member gave the best answers to the interviewer's questions?
   ▶ Did you learn a new answer to a difficult question?
   ▶ What constructive criticism can you provide to each individual?

16. Evaluate your own performance during the role-playing situations.

   ▶ Identify two areas on which you need to improve to have better interviewing skills.
   ▶ What was the most difficult question you were asked? Evaluate your response, and formulate an improved answer.

17. In your assigned team, use your word processing or desktop publishing software to prepare a manual on interviewing that you can use throughout your career. Be sure to include checklists, tips, sample questions an interviewer may ask, sample questions you may ask during an interview, illegal questions, and how to negotiate. Include at least two images in your manual.

   Note: Be sure to make a list of all the tasks your team must perform to prepare the manual. Then assign duties to each team member and develop a time line for completing the work. Remember to include the proofreading and revising stage to finalize the manual.

For your team to work efficiently, prioritize the work and assign tasks to each team member.

Activity 8
Exploring Employment Benefits Packages

While you are still young, you should learn that you are never too young to consider the long-term impact that employment decisions will have on your financial future. With each full-time position and some part-time positions that you encounter, you should explore thoroughly the benefits packages the employer offers.

What is a benefits package? Most companies offer full-time and some part-time employees a **benefits package** that may include an insurance plan for health, life, dental, vision, or disability; profit-sharing plans; retirement plans; paid vacations; paid holidays; education reimbursement plans; bonuses; and many other options. The costs of the benefits package may be paid by the employer or shared between the employer and the employee.

Because benefits packages will vary from one company to another, you should analyze carefully the pay as well as the benefits package when you are offered a job with a company. Don't assume that a higher paying job is better than another job. After you consider the total compensation package (pay plus benefits), you may determine that a slightly lower salary is better for your financial future because of the benefits that accompany the position.

To analyze the options a company offers through what is now called a **cafeteria plan**, employees must consider not only their individual needs but also the needs of their families. For example, if a family has a child or children leave home, the benefits required for the family will change.

After you complete this activity, you will be able to:

- Explain the importance of benefits in the total compensation package.
- Identify specific information about cafeteria plans and employee benefits.
- Identify individual needs and choose employment benefits wisely.
- Prepare a written report about employment benefits.
- Prepare an oral presentation about the benefits a company offers.

To explore information on employment benefits packages, follow these steps:

1. Launch your browser software, and connect to the Internet.

Remember to explore FAQs for additional information.

2. Explore the Internet for information on cafeteria plans at the web sites at these URLs:

Ideal Technical Services	http://www.ideal4u.com/benefits.htm
Workplace Issues	http://www.afscme.org/afscme/wrkplace/cafe.htm
BenefitsLink	http://benefitslink.com/
Dolan Financial Service	http://www.dolanfinancial.com

Figure 2-13 on page 50 shows the BenefitsLink web site.

Figure 2-13
BenefitsLink Web Page

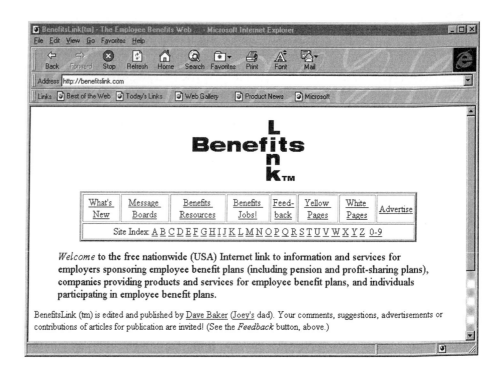

- ▶ What is a cafeteria plan?
- ▶ Why is the term *cafeteria plan* appropriate?
- ▶ What is Section 125?
- ▶ How does a cafeteria plan work?
- ▶ What benefits can be included in a cafeteria plan?
- ▶ What are the possible problems with a cafeteria plan?
- ▶ What is the future of cafeteria plans?

3. As you conduct your research on employee cafeteria plans, link to information that relates to the following list of benefits:

Health	Paid Vacations
Life	Paid Holidays
Dental	Discounts
Vision	Flexible Spending Accounts
Disability	Sick Pay
Profit Sharing	Leave of Absence
Retirement	Bonuses
Education	Travel Expenses
Child Care	

Remember that you can save web pages and review them later while working off-line.

4. Use an Internet search engine to locate additional information about cafeteria benefits packages. You may want to choose a search engine from among the URLs listed below.

AltaVista	http://www.altavista.digital.com/
Lycos	http://www.lycos.com/
Excite	http://www.excite.com/
Magellan	http://www.mckinley.com/
Yahoo	http://www.yahoo.com/

You may want to use **employee cafeteria plans** or **benefits packages** as the keywords in your search.

Note: When you explore a page looking for information on employment benefits packages, look for links that match your search criteria. In your journal record trends for each of the benefits.

5. Search for a company for which you might someday want to work. Locate an e-mail address for the company. Then send an e-mail message to the company to secure information about the benefits the company offers. Be sure to ask whether the company offers a cafeteria plan.

    Note: You may want to use the same company you explored in Activity 7. In your e-mail message you may want to explain that you are conducting research for a school project.

The Deja News Research Service web site is a tool for searching through postings in thousands of newsgroups.

6. Search for a newsgroup that relates to employment practices. Explore for articles related to employee cafeteria plans or benefits packages.

    Note: To find a newsgroup, you may want to go to the Deja News Research Service web site at **http://www.dejanews.com/**

7. Exit your browser software.

Dividing work among team members provides for efficiency.

8. Working in your assigned team, evaluate the information each team member collected about benefits packages and cafeteria plans. Determine whether you need to conduct additional research to address the questions in step 2 and the benefits in step 3. Then develop a work plan for your team to prepare a summary (see step 10) and a table (see step 9) of the information you each gathered. Your work plan should list all the tasks your team must complete, a timetable for completing the tasks, and the team member responsible for each task.

9. Using either your spreadsheet software or the table feature of your word processing or desktop publishing software, prepare a table that summarizes your findings.

    Note: Consider listing the benefit in the first column followed by a brief description of the benefit in the second column. In the third column identify the *pro* or *con* of the benefit as it relates to you. Then include a column for each team member to evaluate the appropriateness of the benefit for the team member at this time in his or her life. Use these ratings for the last column: *2* for very important, *1* for important, *0* for not important.

Remember to check your report carefully for grammar, punctuation, and spelling errors.

10. Using your word processing or desktop publishing software, prepare a report to summarize the information on each of the benefits you explored. Include your table in the report.

11. Prepare notes for an informative oral report on the company you explored in this activity. Using your presentation software, prepare at least three slides to use in your oral report.

Activity 9
Investigating Hiring and Firing Practices

What characteristics do employers look for in prospective employees? What computer skills do employers expect new employees to have? What dress codes do most employers follow? Are companies legally permitted to test for drug use? What management style is practiced by companies? What are the legal issues related to interviewing prospective employees? When you go to any job interview, you should pursue answers to these and other questions so that you can understand clearly the expectations of the prospective employer.

If you do not meet the expectations of an employer, the employer has justifiable reasons to dismiss or fire you from the company. What are the primary reasons businesses fire employees in today's world? Are employees not exhibiting appropriate work habits such as promptness, honesty, accuracy, cooperativeness, and accountability? What are the legal issues related to firing employees?

After you complete this activity, you will be able to:

- Identify legal issues related to hirings and firings.
- Search for information on hiring and firing practices around the world.
- Search for the e-mail addresses of businesses.
- Compose a survey to send to businesses via e-mail.
- Send and read mail messages.
- Compose a written report about your findings on hirings and firings.
- Prepare an oral presentation on your findings.

To learn about the hiring and firing practices of businesses, follow these steps:

1. Launch your browser software, and connect to the Internet.

2. Go to the Smart Business Supersite page at this URL:
   http://www.smartbiz.com/sbs/arts/lll10.htm
   The article at that site provides a legal overview of hiring and firing practices.

   > The last part of this URL has three *l*'s (el's) and one one.

   - Identify the areas an employer should legally avoid during an interview.
   - What is a noncompete document?
   - What is a work for hire?
   - Why should an employer keep complete and accurate records of the behavior and performance of each employee?
   - Identify several justifiable reasons for firing an employee.
   - Identify several factors an employer should consider before firing an employee.

▶ How should an employer handle a termination?
▶ Identify several factors an employer should consider after firing an employee.

3. Use an Internet search engine to locate information on hiring and firing practices in the United States and in the world. You may want to choose a search engine from among the URLs listed below.

AltaVista	http://www.altavista.digital.com/
Lycos	http://www.lycos.com/
Excite	http://www.excite.com/
Magellan	http://www.mckinley.com/
Yahoo	http://www.yahoo.com/

Note: You may want to use **hiring and firing practices** as the keywords in your search. You may also want to narrow your search further by using a career as a keyword.

4. Now locate web sites for at least five companies for which you might someday want to work. Then find an e-mail address for each of the selected companies. Many web pages have an e-mail address link.

▶ Verify that you meet these criteria in your choice of companies:
All companies have positions for which you might someday be prepared.
At least one of the five companies must be in another country.
Three of the companies must be located in different states of the United States.
You have not been employed by any of these companies.

Note: In Activities 7 and 8 you explored for information about a company for which you might someday want to work. You may want to use the e-mail address for that company in this activity.

▶ What are the names of the five companies you want to explore?
▶ List the e-mail address for each of the companies.
▶ Record a brief description of the overall mission of each of the companies.

5. Exit your browser software.

6. Using your word processing software, compose a brief survey that you can send to businesses. Your survey should have an introductory paragraph to explain that you are fulfilling a research project for your high school class. Include three questions related to hiring practices and three questions related to firing practices. Provide a date by which the business should respond; allow about two weeks. Include directions for the recipient to use an appropriate subject line for the reply; for example, Survey—[*Your name*]. Save the survey as a text file so you can upload the file when you compose your mail message to send to the businesses.
Note: Share your survey with a classmate, asking for constructive criticism. You don't want to send a survey with grammar or spelling errors to a business.

7. Launch your browser software.

Remember that you can save web pages and review them later while working off-line.

Be sure to discuss the names of your chosen companies with your teacher before you proceed with this activity.

8. Using your e-mail software, send your survey to each of your five chosen businesses. Use an appropriate subject to attract attention.

9. Exit your browser software.

10. Check your mail for replies on a daily basis. Download the replies.

11. Using your word processing or desktop publishing software, compose a report that summarizes your findings on hirings and firings. You may want to search the Internet for relevant clip art images to include in your report.

Remember to include citations for others' material.

12. In your assigned team, share the results of your research. Then determine an outline to merge the individual reports from each team member to have one complete report of your team's findings on hirings and firings. Be sure to edit the report to eliminate repetitive information. Organize the information to have a logical arrangement. Proofread the report to avoid grammar, spelling, and punctuation errors.

13. Review the final report to determine relevant illustrations to enhance and support the text of your report. Then use appropriate software to prepare the illustrations.
    Note: Always include a reference to an illustration with the text and then label the illustration with the same reference; for example, Figure 1 identifies the percentage of employees in the surveyed businesses who have Internet skills, basic computer skills, and computer programming skills.

14. Prepare appropriate notes for an oral presentation of your team's findings. Using presentation software, prepare at least three slides to use in your oral presentation.
    Note: Be sure to divide the tasks so that each team member has a part in the oral presentation.

Activity 10
Earning Your Wages

In Activity 9 you learned about hiring and firing practices in businesses around the world for which you might someday want to work. What if you actually applied for a job with these companies and you were offered a position? Assuming the employer told you the pay you would receive, would you know how much money you would take home in your paycheck? Do you know how much money the employer would withhold for federal, state, and local taxes?

Employers must adhere to the federal and state tax laws that exist. As a result, employers must withhold payroll deductions for each employee. As a member of the American workforce, you need to know about taxes and net income. You also need to know about the trends in pay raises across the United States.

After you complete this activity, you will be able to:

- Search for federal, state, and local tax information and rates.
- Compose a questionnaire to send to businesses via e-mail.
- Send and read mail messages.
- Create a spreadsheet to compute pay and withholding deductions.
- Create a spreadsheet chart.
- Compose a report on your findings on wages and taxes.
- Share your findings with your team members.

To learn about earning your wages, follow these steps:

1. Launch your browser software, and connect to the Internet.

2. Go to the Payroll Taxes Information Web Site at this URL:
   http://www.payroll-taxes.com/
   Your screen should be similar to the Symmetry web page in Figure 2-14 on page 56. This web site provides information on federal and state taxes. For each state specific information is provided on state and local taxes and state labor laws.

Remember that you can save web pages or print pages for later reference.

3. Explore links for information on federal taxes and state taxes for your individual situation. Record information in your journal, or print web pages for reference when you are off-line.
   - What is the standard deduction for your situation?
   - What is the federal income tax rate that you would pay?
   - What is the FICA wage base and rate?
   - What is the FUTA wage base and rate?
   - What is the 401(k) limit?
   - What is the state income tax rate?
   - What is the local income tax rate?

Figure 2-14
Symmetry's Payroll Taxes
Information Web Page

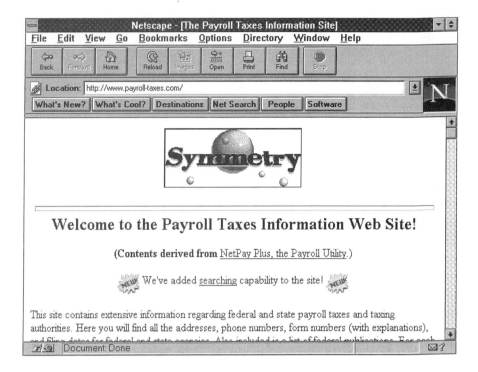

Remember to save to
disk or print any web
pages you may want
to refer to later.

> ▸ Does your location have a school district income tax? If so, what is the rate?
>
> ▸ What is the labor law in your state?

4. Use an Internet search engine to locate additional information on taxes in your state. You may want to choose a search engine from among the URLs listed below.

AltaVista	**http://www.altavista.digital.com/**
Lycos	**http://www.lycos.com/**
Excite	**http://www.excite.com/**
Magellan	**http://www.mckinley.com/**
Yahoo	**http://www.yahoo.com/**

Note: The Infoseek search engine site (**http://www.infoseek.com/**) includes a *Taxes* searching criteria to help you locate information on the Internet.

5. Exit your browser software.

6. In Activity 9 you learned about hiring and firing practices in businesses around the world for which you might someday want to work. You sent an e-mail message to four businesses in the United States. Using your word processing software, compose a questionnaire that you can send via e-mail to each of the four businesses. Your questionnaire should include a brief paragraph that indicates you are conducting research for a high school business course. Your questionnaire should include three to five questions that relate to wages, such as the following:

> ▸ What is the pay for an entry-level position for which you could qualify upon graduation from high school?
>
> ▸ Does the company have a probationary employment time? If so, how long?

- ▶ When can new employees expect a salary review?
- ▶ What is the range for salary increases?

Note: Be sure to include in your questionnaire a date by which you want to receive the company's response; allow about two weeks. Also include specific directions for the recipient to use an appropriate subject line for the reply; for example, Survey—[*Your name*]. Save the questionnaire as a text file so you can upload the file when you compose your mail message to send to the businesses.

7. Launch your browser software, and use your e-mail software to send your questionnaire to each of the four United States' companies you explored in Activity 9. Use an appropriate subject to attract attention. *Note:* You may also want to locate a newsgroup or listserv to which you can send your questionnaire. Confirm with your teacher that you may send the questionnaire to the newsgroup or listserv.

8. Exit your browser software.

9. Check your mail for replies on a daily basis. Download the replies. *Note:* If you do not receive any replies from your e-mail messages within a few days, you may want to search for other e-mail addresses of companies to which you can send your questionnaire. You need to have at least four responses for this activity.

10. Using your spreadsheet software, create a spreadsheet to compute your gross pay and the amount of withholdings for federal, state, and local taxes. Use the amount of pay you learned from the four businesses and the tax rates you learned in your research for this activity. In your spreadsheet, be sure to include a column that identifies the company, the pay, the tax amounts, and the take-home pay (based on these deductions). *Note:* Be sure to include an appropriate spreadsheet title that indicates whether the spreadsheet is based on a weekly, biweekly, or monthly pay period.

11. Create a spreadsheet chart to depict the percentage of withholdings for federal, state, and local taxes for each of the pay situations.

12. Using your word processing or desktop publishing software, compose a report that summarizes your findings on wages and federal, state, and local taxes. You may want to search the Internet for relevant clip art images to include in your report. Include relevant charts to enhance your report.

13. In your assigned team, discuss the value of knowing about federal, state, and local income taxes and other payroll deductions. Discuss the various salary review and salary increase procedures within the companies you explored.

Always send a thank-you message to those who reply to your questionnaire.

Share your report with others, asking for constructive criticism.

Activity 11
Figuring Your Salary

Someday you may want to live on your own. And someday you may have a job in one city and pursue employment opportunities in another city. Would you know how much money you would need to earn in a different location to maintain your same standard of living? What if you had an opportunity to work in a different country? How much would it cost you to move from one location to another?

Moving can be stressful for all concerned. Have you ever moved from one city to another? Would you know how to plan for a geographical relocation?

After you complete this activity, you will be able to:

- Use a salary calculator to compute equivalent salaries in various geographical locations.

- Use a moving calculator to compute the costs associated with moving to different locations.

- Determine a time line for moving from one location to another.

- Create a spreadsheet to depict the salary and moving costs information.

- Compose a summary of the findings of your team.

To learn more about salary calculation and relocation expenses, follow these steps:

1. Launch your browser software, and connect to the Internet.

2. Go to the Homebuyer's Fair web site at this URL:
   http://www.homefair.com
   Your screen should be similar to the Homebuyer's Fair web page in Figure 2-15 on page 59.

3. Link to <u>The Salary Calculator</u>. This page will allow you to compare a particular salary for a given location with the equivalent salary in another geographical location. The cost of living differences between the two locations are considered to determine the salary differences.

4. Follow the directions on this page, and enter a salary that you are presently making or expect to earn as an entry-level employee.
   Note: You may want to refer to your mail replies from Activity 10 for a realistic salary for an entry-level position for which you might someday be able to apply. If you do not know a realistic salary, use **20000**.

5. Using the four locations for jobs that you explored in Activities 9 and 10, enter the appropriate information and calculate the equivalent salaries for the various cities. Record the salaries and locations in your journal.

6. Go back to the Homebuyer's Fair page. Using the location for an international position that you explored in Activity 9, link to the

You may calculate salaries for other cities if you want. If the particular city is not provided in the options, look at a map and find the city that is nearest to your desired location.

Figure 2-15
Homebuyer's Fair Web Page

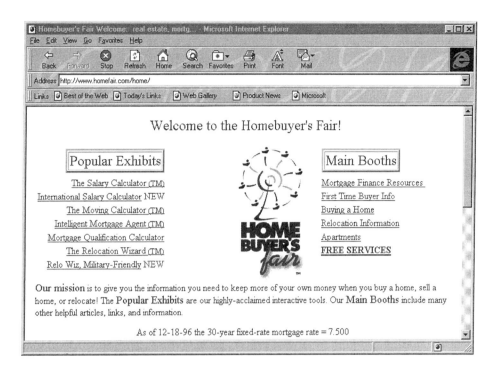

International Salary Calculator. Enter the appropriate information to determine the equivalent salary. Record the salary and the location in your journal.

7. If you have chosen locations that would require you to move, you need to know about the costs associated with moving. Go back to the Homebuyer's Fair page, and link to The Moving Calculator to explore for information on the costs to move to the various locations. Record the information in your journal.

8. Go back to the Homebuyer's Fair page, and link to The Relocation Wizard. (See Figure 2-16 on page 60.) Explore this page to plan a time line for a move to one of your chosen locations. Print the time line.

9. Exit your browser software.

10. Using your spreadsheet software, create a spreadsheet that depicts the initial location and the destination cities, salaries, and percent differences along with the costs to move to the various locations. Analyze your results.

   ▶ Why is the cost of living higher in some locations?
   ▶ Do weather conditions or geography make a difference in the cost of living?
   ▶ Is it more economical to make a move while your salary is lower or to wait until your salary might be in a higher bracket?
   ▶ What can you conclude by studying the time line for a move from one location to another?

11. In your assigned team, share your findings from this activity. Discuss what you learned and how you will be able to use this information and site in your personal, work, and school activities.

Figure 2-16
The Relocation Wizard
Web Page

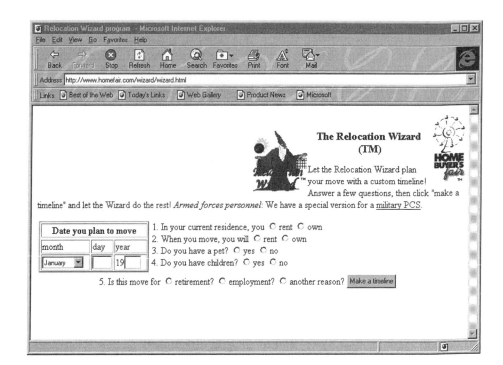

For efficient teamwork, be sure to prioritize the tasks and assign work to each team member.

12. In your assigned team, use your word processing or desktop publishing software to compose a summary of the information your team explored in this activity. Include relevant charts and images to enhance your summary.

Activity 12
Creating Your Own Web Page

As you have visited web pages on the Internet, you have noticed the different elements that appear on the page. You've watched the mouse pointer change from an arrow to a hand whenever you move over some text and pictures. As you know, these hot spots identify links to other pages and web sites. Have you observed the various text styles, fonts, sizes, and color usage on the page. The next time you visit a web page, notice the general layout of information, including the graphic art elements. Look for other user interface controls such as buttons, input fields, pop-up lists, check boxes, and radio buttons.

How are all of these elements combined on a web page? HTML, or Hyper-Text Markup Language, is a standard format comprised of special codes and tags that define how text, pictures, video, and audio occur on a page. An important advantage of HTML is its portability across numerous computer operating systems.

Anyone can create an HTML document using word processing software. Specialized programs are also available that help you build web pages interactively. These tools allow you to see how the page will actually look on the screen when you are finished. Your browser software, in turn, reads the HTML text file, interprets the codes, and displays the information accordingly.

Although mastering HTML requires practice, you can quickly create a simple web page. Once you understand the basic codes and formatting options, enhancements become easier as you gain confidence. You will learn how to format a sample document using the HyperText Markup Language; and then you will prepare the document for the World Wide Web. After you understand the basics, you can format your résumé using HTML. Remember to always put forth your best effort, since anything published on the web is instantly accessible by millions of people around the world.

After you complete this activity, you will be able to:

- Explain basic HTML codes and formatting options.
- Create a web page.
- Edit and revise a web page.
- Upload a web page to an Internet server.
- Import graphics for use on a web page.
- Develop your résumé for publication on the World Wide Web.

To learn more about creating a web page, follow these steps:

1. Launch your browser software, and connect to the Internet.

2. Find several resources on the web that explain how to create basic web pages. Figure 2-17 on page 62 shows some of the information

Figure 2-17
Netscape: How to Create
Web Services Page

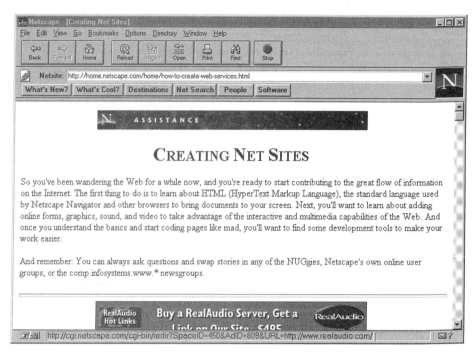

Print or save the information you find and review it off-line. Set bookmarks for those resources that you find especially helpful.

available at the Netscape web site. Carefully review the information provided. Several other resources are listed below:

http://www.ncsa.uiuc.edu/General/Internet/WWW/
   HTMLPrimer.html

http://www.sfsu.edu/training/html.htm

http://www.pcweek.com/eamonn/crash_course.html

http://home.netscape.com/home/how-to-create-web-services.html

3. Use a search engine to locate additional references that explain how to create a web page using the HyperText Markup Language.

4. Exit your browser software.

By choosing to view the source from your browser software, you can see the HTML formatting codes and tags in any web page.

5. Study the materials you have located until you feel comfortable with the basic HTML codes. Access the Internet if you need to find other resources.

6. Using your word processing software, create a new document. Begin by entering the text and HTML codes shown in Figure 2-18 on page 63. Replace the generic text with information about yourself. Keep it simple for your first try.
   Note: Although specialized tools simplify the process of creating web pages, you will learn how to prepare an HTML document using word processing software. If you have access to any of these formatting tools, you can use them to enhance your web page after you complete this activity.

7. Save the document as a text file. If you are working on an IBM (or compatible) computer, name the file **SAMPLE.HTM**. Use the file name

Figure 2-18
Sample HTML Document

```
<HTML>
<HEAD>
<TITLE>Your Name</TITLE>
</HEAD>
<BODY>
<H1>Learning HTML is Fun and Easy!</H1>
<H2>This is a Level 2 Heading.</H2>
<P>This is the first paragraph.</P>
<P>This is the second paragraph.</P>
<P>This is the area where your text goes. Also you may put in
links to other web pages, pictures, tables, and other useful
things.</P>
</BODY>
</HTML>
```

SAMPLE.HTML if you are working on a Macintosh (or compatible) computer. Limit the file name to eight characters plus the extension.

Remember that you should always save an HTML document as an ASCII text file.

8. Quit your word processing software, or close the sample document. Otherwise you may not be able to open it using your browser software.

9. Launch your browser software, but do not connect to the Internet. Open the HTML document you just created. The browser software will read your file, interpret the HTML codes, and display the document as shown in Figure 2-19. It does not matter that the document is stored on your computer or located on a server across the country. You should now see your first web page! Congratulations! Okay, so it's not fancy, but you'll have the opportunity to revise it.

Figure 2-19
Sample HTML Document
Displayed by a Browser
Program

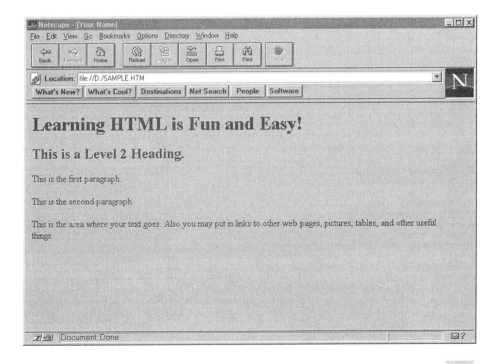

Note: You may have to enter the path and file name to open an HTML document, depending on the browser software. For example, enter **file://C:/SAMPLE.HTM** to open the file if you saved it on Drive C on your Windows-based computer. Access online help and review the steps to open a file from disk if you have difficulties opening your file.

10. Carefully proof your work. Make any necessary changes.

11. *Optional:* Ask your teacher if the Internet service provider your school uses allows students to place web pages on the server. If so, follow the required steps to upload your web page onto the server.

12. Launch your browser software, and enter the URL to open your web page. Proof your work and exit your browser software when you finish.

13. Enhance your web page by adding graphics and hotlinks to other web pages. Proof your work, check it with a browser software off-line, and then upload the file to the server.
    Note: Review the online resources for the HTML codes to include a link to another URL and to show a picture on a web page. Look for the following HTML codes to perform these functions:
    <IMG SRC="picture.extension"> and
    <a href="URL">text of link</a>

14. Working in your assigned team, create a web page that will act as a directory to each student's web page in the class. Every student's web page should include a link to return to the student directory.

You could use a scanner to scan a photograph of yourself and include it in your web page.

15. Prepare a brief demonstration of your project. Select one or more of your team members to demonstrate your web pages to the entire class.

16. Using your word processing software, prepare a résumé and an HTML version of the résumé. Then copy the HTML version to the web.

Activity 13
Protecting Your Computer Against Viruses

What do you know about computer viruses? Let's find out by taking this quiz. Record your responses (true or false) in your journal, and then check your responses after you complete this activity.

Computer Virus Quiz

1. You can get a computer virus by browsing the Internet.
2. You can get a computer virus by reading e-mail sent via the Internet.
3. Viruses only affect program files.
4. You can get computer viruses from data files.
5. You are safe by using only retail software packages.
6. Shareware programs are likely to have viruses.
7. Write-protecting the files on your hard disk prevents viruses.
8. A good virus protection program can protect you from all computer viruses.
9. Viruses always make your hard drive crash.
10. A human can catch a computer virus.

If you have worked with computers for very long, then you have undoubtedly heard about or even experienced computer viruses. These errant programs can erase your hard drive, randomly display unwelcome messages or graphics on your computer screen, and cause other software to malfunction.

Computer viruses spread from one computer to another by reproducing and then infecting other sources. Viruses attach themselves to other programs and even invade computer operating systems. When you run a program with a virus, the virus looks for other programs to infect. Many computer viruses, unfortunately, are not easy to detect. You may unintentionally spread a virus to another computer when you share infected programs or download them from the Internet.

How do you protect your computer against these viruses? Software is available to help prevent computer viruses from infecting your computer. These antivirus programs serve as a sentry to prevent unauthorized access to programs or your operating system. Antivirus programs, available in stores and as shareware, also let you remove a virus or "disinfect" your computer.

After you complete this activity, you will be able to:

- Describe how viruses spread from computer to computer.
- Identify virus protection software programs.
- Download virus protection and disinfectant software.

- Identify several computer viruses and how they work.
- Check computers for viruses.

To learn more about protecting your computer against viruses, follow these steps:

1. Launch your browser software, and connect to the Internet.

You should always check any program that you download from the Internet to make sure that the software does not contain a virus.

2. Go to the Hitchhikers Web Guide AntiVirus Resources page at this URL: **http://www.hitchhikers.net/av.shtml**
   Your screen should be similar to the Hitchhikers Web Guide AntiVirus Resources web page in Figure 2-20. This site is an excellent resource for access to many services, including antivirus shareware, online virus reporting, tools, research papers, and virus lists.

Figure 2-20
Hitchhikers Web Guide
AntiVirus Resources Page

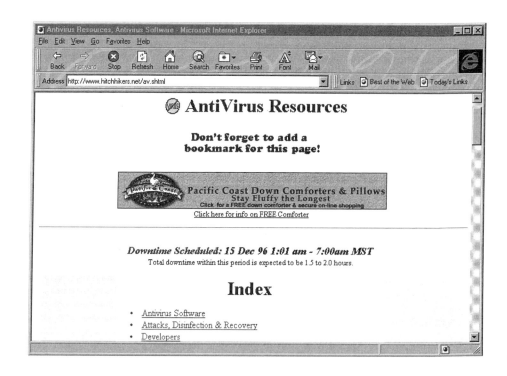

3. Explore this site to locate an antivirus program that is compatible with your Windows 3.1, Windows 95, or Macintosh computer.

4. Download the antivirus software to your computer.

Be sure to ask your teacher for permission before you download any file to your computer.

5. Research at least five known computer viruses. Record the information you find in your journal.
   - What is the name of the virus?
   - Does it infect program files or the operating system?
   - What are the common symptoms?
   - What damage does it cause?
   - How is the virus transmitted to other computers?

6. Continue to explore the links on the Hitchhikers Web Guide AntiVirus Resources page to check your responses to the quiz at the beginning of this activity.

Note: If you can't find the link to the Stiller Research page at the Hitchhikers Web Guide site, you may want to read the information on widespread virus myths at this URL:
http://www.stiller.com/myths.htm

7. Have you or a friend ever encountered a computer virus? If so, search for information on the virus. Learn as much information as you can about the virus.

8. Go back to the Hitchhikers Web Guide AntiVirus Resources page. Locate information that explains what steps you should take to remove a virus. Record any notes in your journal.

   ▶ How many virus protection programs should you have?
   ▶ What are some of the most popular disinfectant programs on the market today?
   ▶ Should you check with antivirus software any software programs that you download from the Internet?
   ▶ What should you do if you encounter a virus that is not on one of the lists?

9. Search for at least two newsgroups that relate to protecting your computers against viruses.
   Note: Ask your teacher whether you may post an article to a newsgroup. If you do have permission, share your article with a classmate for constructive criticism before you post it.

   ▶ Identify the newsgroups you found that relate to computer viruses.
   ▶ What information did you learn by lurking?

Lurking means to read articles in a newsgroup.

10. Exit your browser software.

11. Using your word processing or desktop publishing software, list the steps you should take if your computer is infected with a virus. Prepare a policy manual for your computer lab that will help prevent the spread of computer viruses at your school. Include clip art images as appropriate.

Carefully read the instructions for the antivirus software before you install it on your computers.

12. Use the antivirus software you downloaded (or another program if your teacher recommends one) to check all the computers in your lab for viruses. Remember to check any floppy disks you may have.

Activity 14
Balancing the Federal Budget

In 1996 the federal government spent more than $1.3 trillion. Every year the government must estimate how much revenue it will collect and decide which programs to fund. If spending is greater than revenues, the government creates a deficit and must borrow money to cover the shortfall. While the government can continue to operate with a deficit, extended deficit spending can negatively affect the economy.

Let's explore the federal budget process. From where does this money come? How does the government spend it—on social programs, national parks, defense, education? Should the government raise income taxes to increase revenue? How do government budget decisions affect you?

After you complete this activity, you will be able to:

- Describe the federal budget process.
- List the government's revenue sources and expenditures.
- Attempt to balance the federal budget by completing a form.
- Compose a report.

To learn more about the federal budget process, follow these steps:

1. Launch your browser software, and connect to the Internet.

The Office of Management and Budget (OMB) is part of the Executive Office of the President (EOP).

2. Go to the White House Office of Management and Budget (OMB) home page at this URL: **http://www.whitehouse.gov/WH/EOP/omb** Your screen should be similar to the Office of Management and Budget (OMB) web site in Figure 2-21 on page 69. The OMB helps the president prepare and administer the federal budget. The OMB web site provides many links to information about the budgetary process. Read about the mission of this agency and how the agency is organized.

Remember that you can print or save any charts that appear on a web page.

3. Explore the most recent *Citizens' Guide to the Federal Budget* to learn about the federal budgetary process. Many charts such as the graph shown in Figure 2-22 on page 69 visually review the budget data.
   - What is the budget?
   - What percentage of the national economy is a result of government spending?
   - What are the major government revenue sources?
   - How is the money spent?
   - Does the government operate with a budget deficit or surplus? Explain.

4. Go to the I2020 web site at this URL: **http://www.i2020.net/~bsweb/jsydenst/usbudget.htm** The I2020 is a national service provider of business internetworking services. The web page is designed to help you understand the federal budget process. You can try to balance the budget by increasing and decreasing expenditures.

Figure 2-21

Office of Management and Budget (OMB) Home Page

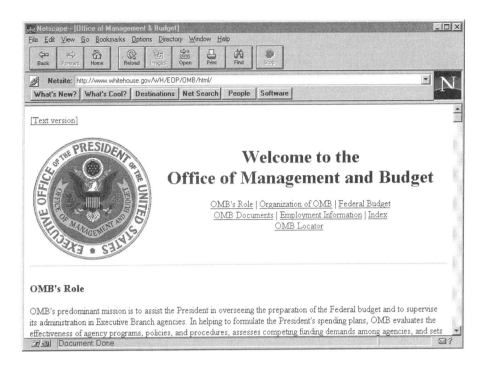

Figure 2-22

Government Revenue Sources

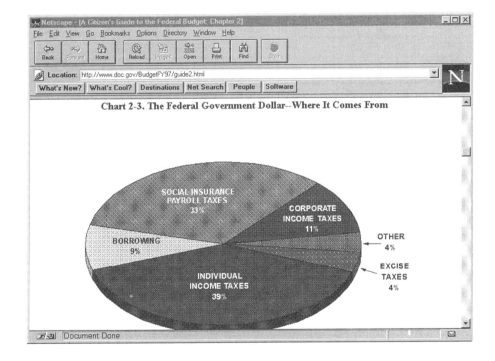

5. Read the instructions about balancing the United States national budget. *Note:* Pay particular attention that all amounts are expressed in billions in the pre-loaded form.

6. Enter the required information for the budget categories and the tax expenditures.

You may want to try several different scenarios to see how changes affect the budget. Can you balance the federal budget?

7. Process the budget information and wait for the results. Print the results.

   ▶ How would you control the federal budget?
   ▶ Where would you increase federal spending? Why?
   ▶ What government spending programs should be reduced? Why?

8. *Optional:* Read the example scenarios at the bottom of the page and perform the calculations.

9. Exit your browser software.

10. Using your word processing or desktop publishing software, compose a report to share your knowledge of the federal budget process. Include clip art images as appropriate. Include relevant charts to support your report.

Activity 15
Discovering How Software is Written

Have you ever wondered what actually makes a software program work? How does a software program display text and pictures on the screen? How does a word processor open a file or print a document? What programming is required for a spreadsheet application to calculate a formula or to chart some data? Seemingly simple programs, such as your browser software, require thousands and often millions of lines of programming code.

If you have ever taken a programming course, you can appreciate the work required to create a computer program that performs even simple tasks. Although you don't need to know programming to use a computer, understanding how software is written may help you use a computer more efficiently.

After you complete this activity, you will be able to:

- Download and uncompress a file.
- Better understand the efforts that go into writing a software program.
- Enhance an existing BASIC software program.
- Develop a flowchart to outline your software program.
- Create a simple program using the BASIC programming language.
- Develop a documentation manual to support your software program.

To discover how software is written, follow these steps:

1. Launch your browser software, and connect to the Internet.

2. Go to the Ainsworth Computer Seminar site at this URL:
   gopher://www.qwerty.com:80/hGET%20/apbook.htm
   Your screen should be similar to the Ainsworth Computer Seminar web page in Figure 2-23 on page 72. This site provides both a quick overview along with detailed information to help you learn more about how software is written. Several sample programs demonstrate fundamental programming techniques, and flowcharts help you visualize how the programs operate.

   Important: Although the program examples are written in Microsoft QBASIC for Windows, the information at this site is also helpful for Macintosh users. You can download the program samples, however, only if you are working on a Windows-based computer and have QBASIC.
   Note: Macintosh users should skip to step 5.

3. Ask your teacher for permission before downloading any program files from the Internet. Then download the complete seminar and its program files to your computer if you are working on a Windows-based computer. The program files contain the sample programming code that appears throughout the tutorial.

> **The URL for the Ainsworth Computer Seminar indicates that this is a gopher site.**

Figure 2-23
Ainsworth Computer
Seminar Page

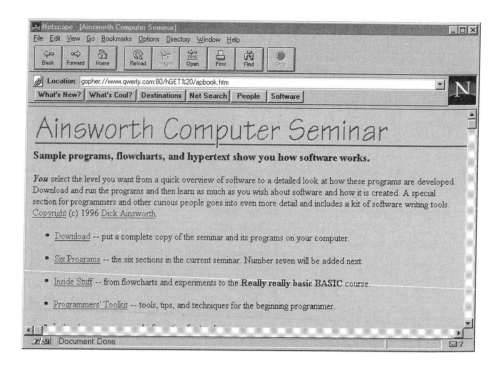

4. Uncompress (unzip) the file you just downloaded. Refer to the instructions provided at the Ainsworth Computer Seminar site if you need help with this process.

   Warning: You should have virus protection software on your computer if you download shareware programs from the Internet and then run them on your system. Refer to Activity 13 for information on protecting your computer against viruses.

5. Since you just downloaded all of the web pages from the Ainsworth Computer Seminar site, you can work off-line if you are using a Windows-based computer. Macintosh users should stay connected and continue with the next step. Disconnect from the Internet, but do not quit your browser software. Open the STARTACS.HTM file from disk using your browser software.

6. Link to <u>Inside Stuff</u>. This page contains other links that provide a basic introduction to programming. Thoroughly explore this area of the Ainsworth Computer Seminar site. Focus on these topics:

   <u>Flowcharts</u>
   <u>Really really basic BASIC</u>
   <u>Programmers' Toolkit</u>

7. Complete either of the experiments presented—Exploring Random Numbers or Exploring Time with Your Computer.

8. Go back to the Ainsworth Computer Seminar home page, and link to the sample programs and flowcharts page. Read about each of the sample programs listed below.

Intro to Isaac	Hangperson
Space Dock	Music Composer
Newtona 500	Simon Sings

If you need assistance, refer to the Really really basic BASIC information.

9. Thoroughly explore the Intro to Isaac program. Review the flowcharts, see how it runs, take an inside look, and examine the programming toolkit.
Note: Remember that you need Microsoft QBASIC to open the source code files.

10. After you understand how the Intro to Isaac program works, modify the program to add one or two enhancements, such as new sounds or color.

11. Explore and enhance one of the other sample programs.

12. Create a new program from scratch. Choose from among the ideas listed below, or select another programming idea.

    Interest Calculator—Accept input for the following: loan amount, interest rate per year, and loan period (years). Then compute the total interest, and display the results.

    Screen Saver—Completely erase the screen, display a message (e.g., your name, school name, and so on) anywhere on the screen, wait a few seconds, erase the message, and then redraw it somewhere else on the screen. Repeat the process until any key is pressed.

    Music Box—Play different notes based on keyboard input. Make sure that your computer has sound capabilities before beginning this project.

13. Prepare a flowchart that outlines how your program will operate. Carefully proof the steps before you begin programming.

Be sure to add comments to your program. Comments help you understand your code, especially if you want to change it later.

14. Using Microsoft QBASIC, write the program. Debug (test) the program to verify that it works properly.

15. Share your software program with a classmate. Secure constructive criticism, and revise your program, if necessary.

16. Using your word processing or desktop publishing software, develop a documentation manual to accompany your software program. Include clip art images as appropriate.

17. Demonstrate the program to your class.
Note: Consider whether you want to use presentation software slides when you demonstrate your software program. You may want to show the class the flowchart that outlines how your program operates.

Activity 16
Publishing on the Web

What's new and interesting at your school? How about sharing that information with others in the community, your state, or even the world—via the Internet? Let's learn how to publish something on the Internet. What better topic to write about than your school—the activities, sports, upcoming events, and school news. Wouldn't you enjoy reading school newsletters from other parts of the country and from around the globe?

After you complete this activity, you will be able to:

- Gather ideas from existing school web pages.
- Develop and use special formatting techniques to create web pages.
- Plan and design the layout for an online newsletter.
- Compose a newsletter to publish on the Internet.
- Write, debug, and implement a web site.

To publish a school newsletter on the Internet, follow these steps:

1. Launch your browser software, and connect to the Internet.

2. Go to the Web66 home page at this URL:
   http://web66.coled.umn.edu/
   Your screen should be similar to the Web66 web page in Figure 2-24.

Figure 2-24
Web66 Home Page

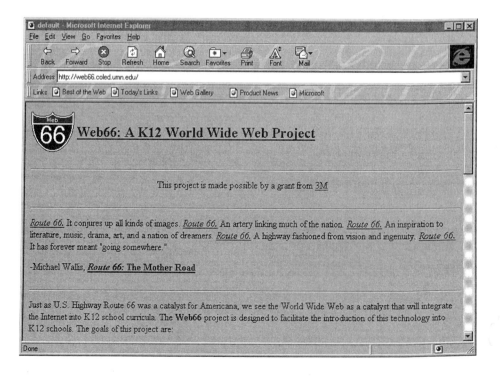

Review the goals of the Web66 project. This site provides information for educators and students to learn about the Internet. Through its international registry, Web66 promotes cooperation among schools. And it offers information on many different Internet resources.

3. Link to the International WWW Schools Registry page. From this page, explore several school web sites in your state and across the nation. Specifically look for web sites that include pages created by high school students. A sample school web site is shown in Figure 2-25.

Figure 2-25
Eisenhower High School
Home Page

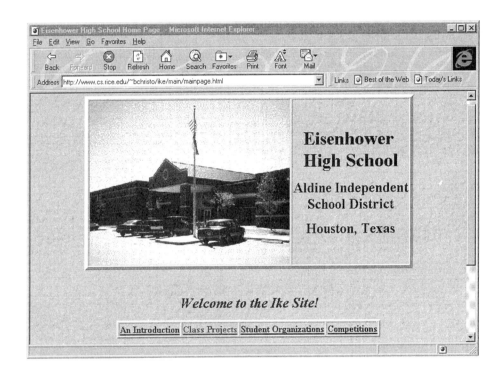

Save or print those web pages that you find interesting or helpful. Remember you can also view the HTML codes on any web page.

4. Gather ideas that will help you publish a school newsletter on the Internet.

5. From the Web66 site, link to school web sites in other countries.
   ▸ What differences exist between the United States sites and the international sites you visited?
   ▸ What kinds of information did the international sites include?
   ▸ Did you have problems displaying pages from non-English speaking countries?

6. Visit some online newspapers and magazines. Look at the layout, graphic elements, advertisements, and links. One popular online newspaper you may want to explore is *USA Today* at this URL: **http://www.usatoday.com/**

7. Exit your browser software.

Use some of the ideas from other sites to plan the design and layout of your newsletter.

8. Working with other team members, plan the design and layout for your school's online newsletter.

Consider the layout for your newsletter as you write so that the copy fits in the space allowed. Remember that numerous online sources exist for clip art.

9. Using your word processing or desktop publishing software, write the content for the newsletter. Assign each team member to cover a different area: upcoming events, sports news, academics, clubs and organizations, and other school news.

10. Using your word processing software or another tool, create the web pages for your newsletter. Format the pages using the proper HTML codes, and save the files to disk. Use clip art, take pictures with a digital camera, or scan photos to add graphics to your web pages.

    Several online resources including those listed below explain how to create web pages. You may want to review some of the more advanced HTML formatting techniques such as headings, paragraphs, lines, lists, links, tables, backgrounds, and images.

    http://www.ncsa.uiuc.edu/General/Internet/WWW/
       HTMLPrimer.html
    http://www.sfsu.edu/training/html.htm
    http://www.pcweek.com/eamonn/crash_course.html
    http://home.netscape.com/home/how-to-create-web-services.html
    http://hakatai.mcli.dist.maricopa.edu/tut/lessons.html

    Note: You may also want to review your work in Activity 12—Creating Your Own Web Page.

11. Launch your browser software, but do not connect to the Internet.

12. Using your browser software, thoroughly test your newsletter off-line. Proof for spelling, punctuation, and grammar errors; review the layout of text and pictures; and check each URL link.

13. Upload the newsletter web pages to your school's web site. Be sure to discuss this process with your teacher, network administrator, or Internet service provider. Add the necessary links from your school's home page to the newsletter. Verify that a link exists to return to the home page.

14. Carefully check the newsletter now that you have installed it on the server. Make any corrections as needed.

15. Demonstrate the newsletter to your teacher and school administrators.

16. Go to the Web66 web site and check to see if your school is included in the registry. If not, register the web site for your school.
    Note: Ask your teacher for permission to do this.

Activity 17
Using an Intranet

Businesses around the world are becoming more and more dependent on computer technology. Many are choosing to set up intranets to distribute information online. As its name implies, an **intranet** is a private network. Intranets and the Internet function in similar ways; but unlike the Internet, access to an intranet is limited only to certain groups. For example, a company may set up an intranet to disseminate employee benefits information, job postings, and other confidential data. Anyone who has the proper access can use browser software to navigate the intranet, just as one would explore information on the World Wide Web.

Intranets offer many advantages not possible with the traditional forms of distribution. Since electronic distribution significantly reduces printing and photocopying expenses, businesses can save money by delivering information online instead of using paper documents. More timely information helps improve productivity when it can be communicated instantly to everyone across an intranet.

How could your school benefit from using an intranet? Think about the advantages to your school. The acceptable use policy, the student handbook, code of conduct, student schedules, cafeteria menu, library schedule, class notes, and any other information could be posted online. With proper planning, an intranet would soon become an important tool for teachers, students, and parents.

After you complete this activity, you will be able to:

- Locate information online about intranets.
- Plan and design the layout for an intranet.
- Implement an intranet.
- Develop a schedule to update an intranet.
- Develop a flyer to announce an intranet.
- Send an e-mail message to announce an intranet.
- Compose a report about careers related to intranet web pages.

To learn more about intranets, follow these steps:

1. Launch your browser software, and connect to the Internet.
2. Go to a commercial search engine to find information that explains how to plan and design an intranet. Consider these URLs for search engines:

AltaVista	**http://www.altavista.digital.com/**
Lycos	**http://www.lycos.com/**
Excite	**http://www.excite.com/**
Magellan	**http://www.mckinley.com/**
Yahoo	**http://www.yahoo.com/**

Set a bookmark if you
identify a helpful site.
Then return to it later to
continue your research.

Locate articles that describe how intranets benefit companies, schools, and other organizations. Note the sample Yahoo Search Results page in Figure 2-26.

Figure 2-26
Yahoo Search Results Page

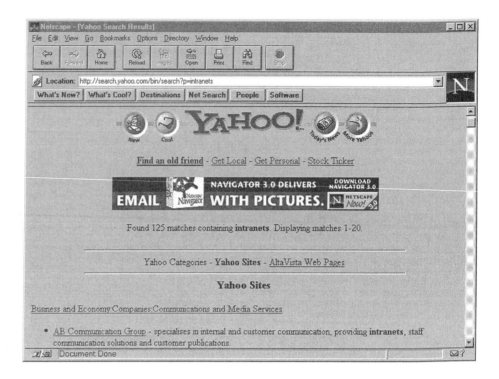

3. Save or print any information that may help you design an intranet for your school. You can review the information off-line as you work on this activity.

4. Exit your browser software.

5. Working in your assigned team, plan interview questions about an intranet that each team member can ask students, parents, teachers, and administrators. Ask questions to determine what kinds of online information would be helpful to them. Develop a plan to conduct the interviews, and then conduct the interviews regarding your intranet plans. Record your findings in your journal.
   Note: Assign each team member particular groups of individuals to interview. For instance, one or two team members might interview teachers, while another team member might interview school administrators. You may also want to explore developing a survey to send to e-mail addresses of individuals related to the school (students, parents, teachers, and so on).

6. Based on the results of your analysis, work as a team to design an intranet for your school. Decide what information should be made available. How much detail should you provide? Be creative with your design. Add pictures and color to enhance the layout.

Note: Divide the project into smaller tasks. For example, one member of the team should plan the home page. Assign other team members to focus on particular areas such as those listed below. You may want to limit the scope of this project to only a few of the areas. Later you can expand the intranet. Gather the information you need.

Home Page   School Calendar
Acceptable Use Policy Who to Contact
Student Handbook   Sporting Events
What's New   Clubs & Organizations

7. As a team, present your design plans to your teacher.

8. Using your word processing software or another tool, create the web pages for your intranet.

Several resources available on the web explain how to create web pages. Several of these resources are listed below.

http://www.ncsa.uiuc.edu/General/Internet/WWW/
    HTMLPrimer.html
http://www.sfsu.edu/training/html.htm
http://www.pcweek.com/eamonn/crash_course.html
http://home.netscape.com/home/how-to-create-web-services.html

Figure 2-27 shows some of the information available at the Netscape web site.

Note: You may also want to review your work in Activity 12—Creating Your Own Web Page and Activity 16—Publishing on the Web.

Figure 2-27
Netscape: How to Create
Web Services Page

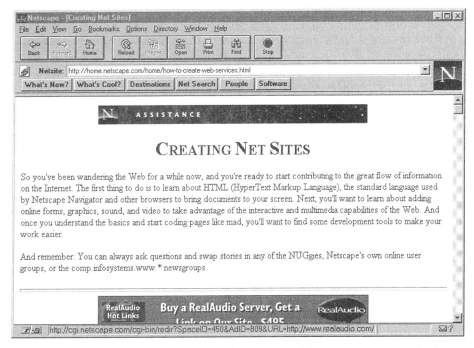

Copyright 1996 Netscape Communications Corp. All Rights Reserved. This page may not be reprinted or copied without the express written permission of Netscape.

Ask a classmate to test your intranet. Secure constructive criticism.

9. Using your browser software, thoroughly test your intranet off-line. Proof for spelling, punctuation, and grammar errors; review the layout of text and pictures; and check each URL link.

10. Explore the security issues needed to protect an intranet. If you cannot provide for a secure site, make sure that you do not include any confidential information.

11. Upload the intranet web pages to the server.
Note: Be sure to discuss this process with your teacher, network administrator, or Internet service provider.

12. Carefully check the intranet now that you have installed your web pages on the server. Make any corrections as needed.

13. Demonstrate the intranet to your teacher and school administrators. Determine the topics to include in your demonstration.
Note: Consider whether you want to use any visual aids during your demonstration.

14. After you receive approval for the intranet, use your word processing or desktop publishing software to develop a flyer to announce the new intranet to teachers, students, parents, school administration, and the community. Be sure to provide the necessary information (URL, password, and so on) to access it.
Note: You may also want to locate e-mail addresses to which you can send the announcement. Explore to see whether a listserv exists that you can use.

Secure approval for your plan to update the intranet from a school administrator.

15. Using your spreadsheet software, develop a schedule for updating the intranet. Most pages will likely stay the same for about a month or so. You might need to update other pages on a weekly basis. Set up a schedule for updating the intranet, and be sure to work with the network administrator.
Note: As you develop a schedule, remember to also assign individuals to update particular pages. Determine whether your school wants to approve all updates.

16. Now that you have developed a web page for your school intranet, explore the Internet for career opportunities related to working on intranet web pages. Using your word processing or desktop publishing software, compose a report about careers and positions that require an individual to work on intranet web pages.

Activity 18
Connecting to a Network

Cables, connectors, and wires extend from one end of a building to the next. Sometimes twisted and tangled, these connections link one computer to another computer to form a **local area network** (**LAN**). These networks have become an integral part of everyday operations for many businesses around the world. Companies rely on this technology to share expensive peripherals and to facilitate the flow of information.

With the increased use of local area networks, the demand for qualified network administrators and network specialists has also increased. These positions are critical in both small and large businesses to keep information flowing throughout the organization. As business requirements change, these individuals plan, design, and implement new systems. They also participate in choosing which topology or configuration is appropriate, provide assistance when installing new systems, and work towards maintaining a system.

After you complete this activity, you will be able to:

- Identify major network hardware and software manufacturers.
- Identify common local area network configurations.
- Identify networking cables and connections.
- Sketch the topology of the network at your school.
- Conduct a survey of businesses that have a LAN.
- Design a new local area network.
- Create a spreadsheet to calculate the costs of a LAN.
- Prepare a proposal for your newly designed LAN.

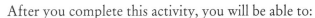

To learn more about local area networks, follow these steps:

1. Launch your browser software, and connect to the Internet.

2. Go to a commercial search engine site to find information about various network topologies. You may want to use one of these search engines:

AltaVista	http://www.altavista.digital.com/
Lycos	http://www.lycos.com/
Excite	http://www.excite.com/
Magellan	http://www.mckinley.com/
Yahoo	http://www.yahoo.com/

Set a bookmark if you identify a helpful site. Then return to it later to continue your research.

3. Identify some of the major network hardware and software manufacturers. Using the Internet, gather information about their products. Figure 2-28 on page 82 shows the Bay Networks home page. Some of the other companies that offer network products include the following:

Cisco Systems	Novell
Lucent Technologies	3Com

Ring, bus, and star configurations represent some of the more common network topologies.

Figure 2-28
Bay Networks Home Page

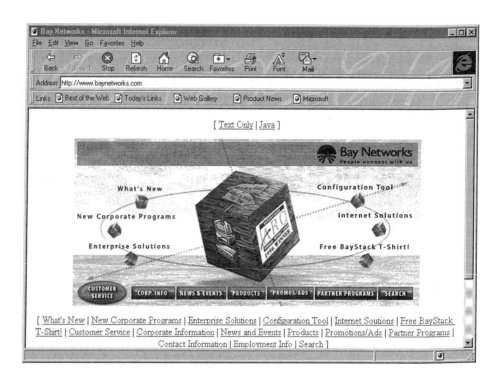

4. Research "wireless" network configurations.
   ▸ Are "wireless" networks possible today?
   ▸ What hardware is required for a wireless network?
   ▸ Do these systems cost more or less than networks connected with cables?
   ▸ What are the advantages and disadvantages of a wireless network?

5. Exit your browser software.

6. Visit your school or public library to reference several computer mail order catalogs. Look at the networking/communications sections of these catalogs.
   ▸ Identify the kinds of cables, cards, and other peripherals needed to set up a LAN.
   ▸ Make a list of the network hardware available.
   ▸ Note the costs for this equipment.

7. *Optional:* If the computers at your school are already networked, sketch the topology, or layout, of the network. A sample diagram that shows a star network topology is illustrated in Figure 2-29 on page 83. Identify all of the hardware components of the local area network at your school.

Before conducting your survey of local businesses, carefully plan your questions and topics.

8. For additional research, conduct a survey of the businesses in your area that have a LAN installed at their facility. Focus on topics such as the following:

Topology	Training
Maintenance	Productivity
Security	Uses

Figure 2-29
Star Network Topology

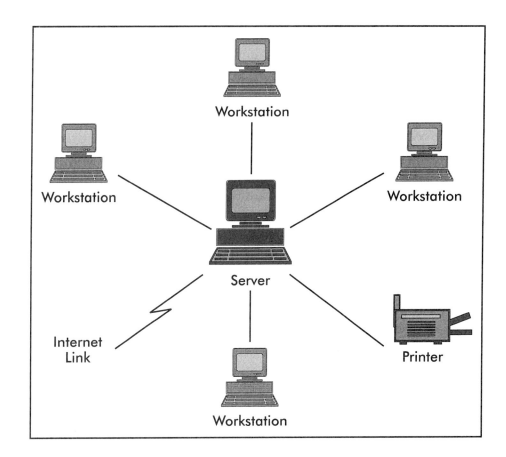

Workstation

Workstation

Workstation

Server

Internet
Link

Printer

Workstation

Note: Check with your teacher to determine which businesses you should visit. Your teacher may assign you to a team to conduct these surveys.

9. Based on the information you have gathered, design a network for your classroom using state-of-the-art equipment. Include the following information:

   Network Layout—Use your paint program, illustration software, or paper and pencil to sketch the layout of the network.

   Equipment Requirements—List all of the equipment (computers, cables, cards, server, and so on) needed to build a network with twenty workstations. Using your word processing software, record this information.

   Costs—Using your spreadsheet software, create a spreadsheet to calculate the cost of the network. Remember to include installation costs.

10. Using your word processing or desktop publishing software, prepare a proposal to your teacher that presents your newly designed LAN and the research data about LANs. Include any images and sketches, reports, and spreadsheets to support your conclusions.

Remember to proofread your document for grammar, spelling, and punctuation errors. Consider asking a classmate for constructive criticism.

Activity 19
Using a Web Video Camera

Did you know that you can actually control a video camera hundreds or even thousands of miles away using your computer and Internet browser software? Web sites such as those at Warp, Ltd. and the University of Chicago are set up to send live video images from a remote location to your computer. After you connect to one of these sites, you can use your browser software to control a telerobotic camera. By simply clicking your mouse, you can direct the camera to zoom in and out, move up or down, and pan left or right. Live video is sent directly to your computer.

Similar technology enables you to use your computer for video conferencing. Equipped with a small camera and the appropriate software, you could use the Internet to send and receive video. Although most computers are not equipped with the necessary high-speed Internet connections to offer broadcast-quality images, hardware and software compression improvements promise better quality in the future.

After you complete this activity, you will be able to:

- Explain how to control a telerobotic camera.
- Operate a remote video camera.
- Discuss potential uses for remote cameras.
- Explore web camera sites.
- Compose a report.
- Prepare a proposal to purchase a telerobotic camera for your school.

To learn more about the Internet and web cameras, follow these steps:

1. Launch your browser software, and connect to the Internet.

2. Go to the Warp, Ltd. web site at this URL: **http://www.warp.com/** After you connect to this site, link to the Webcam demo page. (See Figure 2-30 on page 85.) Review the information that explains how this technology works.

View sites with video cameras at different times of the day to see how the images change.

3. Link to the Webcam demo. Then use your mouse to try to move the camera. Click on the left edge of the picture, and wait while the updated image is sent to your computer. Try to move the camera in other directions.

4. Go to the University of Chicago Computer Science Department "labcam" web site at this URL: **http://vision.cs.uchicago.edu/cgi-bin/labcam/** Click anywhere on the image to aim the telerobotic camera at that point. Then wait while the image is updated.
   - Does this camera operate differently than the VTV Webcam?
   - What are the differences, if any?
   - Can you control other functions of the camera? How?

Figure 2-30
Warp, Ltd. Webcam Page

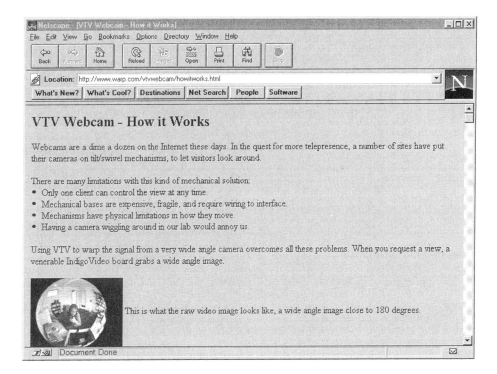

Telerobotic cameras are growing rapidly in popularity and are used for indoor surveillance, traffic updates, and just for fun.

5. Go to The Web Voyeur home page at this URL:
   http://pobox.com/~voyeur/
   If a site you want to explore is no longer available, try some of the many others listed at The Web Voyeur site. This site includes an up-to-date list of live video views available on the web.

6. Explore at least three web camera sites. Compare and contrast the different sites. Visit the sites at different times of the day to see how the images are updated.

7. Exit your browser software.

8. Using your word processing software, compose a report that presents your findings on web video cameras.
   ▸ How do telerobotic cameras operate?
   ▸ What are some of the more interesting sites you visited?
   ▸ What are the potential uses of this new technology?

Include appropriate citation of others' information.

9. Using your word processing or desktop publishing software, prepare a proposal to your teacher to purchase a telerobotic camera for your computer lab. Discuss the following issues:
   Hardware Requirements
   Software Requirements
   Costs and Funding
   Installation
   Maintenance
   ▸ Include relevant images and information to support your proposal.

10. In your assigned team, prepare a multimedia presentation to your school administration to demonstrate using a web video camera. Include appropriate presentation slides and visual aids to use as hand-outs during your presentation.

Activity 20
Exploring Emerging Technologies

Do you remember the first time you heard about the Internet? Has the power of the Internet and other technologies impressed you? While you may not have been around when electricity was discovered, you have probably seen a myriad of revolutionary changes that affect everyday life. Many of these new technologies simplify our lives; many help us to be more productive citizens and employees.

Can you predict what changes new technology will bring to your life? How will it affect you at school, at home, and at work? Will it change the way schools and colleges approach education? How will companies conduct business in the future? Is the Internet here to stay? Certainly new technology will impact our lives. Let's explore some of the latest technology in areas such as business, education, medicine, and robotics.

After you complete this activity, you will be able to:

- Work with team members to select a research project.
- Research emerging technologies.
- Prepare a slide show.
- Prepare a summary.
- Present your findings.
- Lead a class discussion about your research project.

To learn more about emerging technologies, follow these steps:

1. In your assigned team, choose a topic in which to explore emerging technologies. If you choose medicine, for example, you will research how new technology will impact surgical techniques, cancer treatment, and drug research. What tools will doctors use to make earlier diagnoses of diseases? How will physicians interact with patients?

   Note: You may choose any area of interest to your team. Your teacher may suggest topics, or you may consider the following list of topics.

Business	Government
Communication	Manufacturing
Computers	Medicine
Education	Robotics
Energy	Transportation

2. Launch your browser software, and connect to the Internet.

3. Begin your search by going to an Internet search engine, such as one of those listed below.

AltaVista	**http://www.altavista.digital.com/**
Lycos	**http://www.lycos.com/**
Excite	**http://www.excite.com/**

Magellan   http://www.mckinley.com/
Yahoo   http://www.yahoo.com/

Review the online help at the search engine to learn how to use the search tool effectively. Figure 2-31 shows the online help for the AltaVista search engine.

Figure 2-31
AltaVista Online Help Page

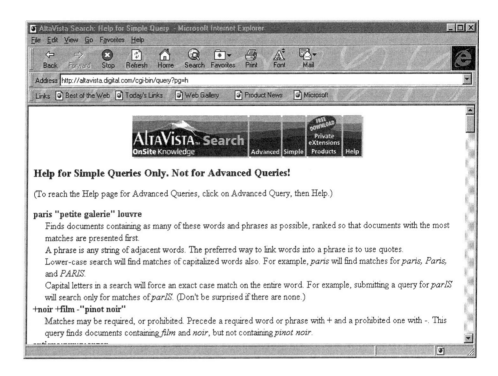

Try using several different keywords and employing Boolean search techniques to help you find information for your research project.

Prioritize the list of resources and assign work to individuals to help your team work efficiently.

Go also to university web sites to determine on what related research projects the faculty and students are working.

4. Each team member should conduct a search related to your topic and make a list of the web sites that are appropriate for your chosen topic. Record the URLs for the web sites in your journal.

5. In your team, review all the sites the team members identified. Merge the individual lists into a single master list. Then prioritize the search work, determining the sites your team should explore further. Assign sites to individuals to explore.
Note: Be sure to establish a time schedule on which all team members will conduct their research on emerging technology. Discuss also whether you should save to disk or print relevant information (including images) you find during the searching process.

6. As you conduct research, identify several companies that do business in the area you selected. Look for larger companies and for entrepreneurial startups. Visit their web sites (if available), and explore the new products they offer. Send e-mail messages as appropriate to gather additional information.
Note: Be sure to make appropriate notes in your journal or save to disk relevant information for use in your team's presentation.

7. Exit your browser software.

8. In your assigned team, share the results of your search. Then determine which sites your team should explore further.

9. Using the resources you identified, gather additional information online. Record notes in your journal, save interesting web pages, or print relevant information.

10. As a team, organize your research results for your presentation to the class. Use your word processing or desktop publishing software to summarize your research findings.
    Note: Remember to delegate responsibilities to all team members.

11. Using your presentation software, prepare at least eight slides for your presentation to the class. Outline your findings. Include clip art and other images to enhance the slides.

12. Use your word processing software to prepare a summary of your findings. Be sure to include information such as the following:
    ▶ What new technology is just on the horizon?
    ▶ How will it affect our lives?
    ▶ What are its uses?
    ▶ What are the advantages and disadvantages of this new technology?
    ▶ How will technology impact us five, ten, or even twenty years from now?

13. Share the summary with each team member to critique for improvements.
    Note: Be sure to correct all grammar, punctuation, and spelling errors.

14. Revise the summary as appropriate.

15. As a team, present your findings to the class. Following your presentation, encourage class discussion related to the new technology.
    Note: Assign a responsibility to each team member so that all participate in the team presentation. Remember to choose a team leader for the presentation and discussion.

▼ Your Portfolio Project

As you complete the many different Internet activities in this book, you will have an opportunity to:

- Learn and apply advanced telecommunications skills.
- Gain new knowledge about personal, local, state, national, and international business topics.
- Develop critical thinking, communication, and teamwork skills as you apply emerging technologies in workplace business situations.

Your completed work on each activity will often include printouts from web pages, reports you compose about the information you explored on the Internet, and printouts using other applications, such as word processing, desktop publishing, spreadsheet, database, and presentation software.

What is a Portfolio?

How will you show other students, teachers, parents, and prospective employers what you have learned about the Internet? How will you demonstrate your knowledge of and ability to use applications software? You can create and build a portfolio. A **portfolio** is a collection of your work that represents what you have learned during this course. Your portfolio should contain samples in a folder that demonstrate the various skills and objectives you have mastered over time as well as samples from individual and team projects.

How Should I Organize My Portfolio?

You can organize your portfolio in a manner that best represents your personality, your work, and your knowledge. Consider these options:

- You can organize the results from all the activities in the order in which you completed the activities. In this arrangement you would demonstrate your progress in learning Internet skills over time.
- You can organize the results from the activities with related materials grouped together. For instance, you would group all material related to the employment process, such as your career plan, your résumé, a web version of your résumé, a letter of application, a follow-up letter, a manual on interviewing, a report on benefits packages, a report on hiring and firing, a report on wages and taxes, and a summary depicting equivalent salaries. In this arrangement you would demonstrate not only the telecommunications and applications software skills you have mastered but also the new knowledge you have acquired on a particular topic.
- You can organize the results from the activities with materials using various applications software grouped together. For instance, you would

group all database activities, all spreadsheet activities, and so on. This arrangement would demonstrate the applications software skills you have mastered.

How Do I Use My Portfolio?

Once you have created your portfolio, don't put it aside. Use your portfolio in these ways:

- Periodically *reflect on* the material in your portfolio. Reflect on what you learned from the activities and how you could improve on future work related to the same topic and telecommunications and applications software skills.

- *Build* your portfolio. Building your portfolio should be a creative, learning process that allows you to collect and select work related to the Internet and applications software.

- *Show* your portfolio to other students, your parents or guardian, other teachers, and prospective employers. Let the world see how you are learning new knowledge and skills to be a productive member of the workforce.

Accept the challenge of being responsible for your own learning. And learn from all your work on the Internet!

▶ **Part**

One Two Three

123

Glossary

Glossary

A

Acceptable Use Policy
AUP; a written contract between a school, a student, and the student's parents or guardian that identifies the rules and guidelines for using the Internet.

Address
See *E-mail address*.

Anonymous FTP
A service provided on some computers that lets you connect to certain remote computers and download files from large databases and archive sites without being a registered user. You generally must use the password *guest* or *anonymous*. (See *FTP*.)

ARPANET
An early network of computer networks funded by the United States Department of Defense Advanced Research Projects Agency (ARPA); the predecessor of the Internet.

ASCII
American Standard Code for Information Interchange; a collection of public domain character sets considered standard throughout the computer industry.

B

Bits per Second
bps; a measurement of telecommunications speed.

Bookmark
A feature of a browser that flags the location of a document. (See *Browser* and *Hot List*.)

Browser
A special software program required to navigate the World Wide Web that allows you to access information on the Internet. (See *Graphical Browser* and *Text Browser*.)

Bulletin Board System
BBS; a central computer used by special interest groups to exchange information on a particular topic. You can connect to a BBS through a phone line, your own computer, and a modem. Most BBSs offer files, programs, and other information that you can download to your own computer; some enable you to send e-mail and chat with other users who are connected at the same time.

C

Client
A term used to describe a computer connected to the Internet that has the capability to share information on the Internet.

com
A top-level domain that means commercial service. (See *Domain Extension*.)

Compressed Files
The format of many files on the Internet. Compressed files use less space than the original files and take less time to download than uncompressed files. To use a compressed file, you must first uncompress it via a special program.

Cyberspace
A term that means the electronic world of the Internet or the World Wide Web. (See *Information Superhighway*.)

D

Dedicated Internet Connection
A connection to the Internet that is active all the time through a permanent link to another Internet service provider.

Dial-up Internet Connection
A connection to the Internet that is active only while you are connected to an Internet service provider through your own computer and modem over a phone line.

Domain
The part of an Internet e-mail address after the @ symbol that identifies the computer where the user is working. For example, in billg@microsoft.com, *microsoft.com* is the domain. (See *Domain Name System*,

E-Mail Address, Subdomain, and Username.)

Domain Extension
Also called the **top-level domain**; the last three letters of an Internet address. Common domain extensions are *.com* for commercial service, *.edu* for education, *.gov* for government, *.mil* for military, *.net* for network provider, and *.org* for organization. A geographical top-level domain identifies a country on the Internet. For example, *us* represents United States, *at* represents Australia, and *ca* represents Canada.

Domain Name System
DNS; the system used to identify Internet addresses. An Internet address consists of a username and domain. (See *Domain*, *Domain Extension*, *E-Mail Address*, and *Username*.)

Download
To copy information or a file from a remote computer to a location on the user's local computer. (See *Upload*.)

E

Electronic Mail
Also called **e-mail**; the transfer of information from one computer to another in electronic format. Users can send text-based messages as well as multimedia documents. Typically, e-mail messages are stored safely in the recipient's electronic "mailbox" until the recipient reads them. Thus, the sender and the recipient need not be using the Internet at the same time.

E-Mail Address
A unique address that identifies you when you are connected to the Internet. Your e-mail address allows you to access information, and others may send information to your address. An e-mail address may be numeric, alphabetic, or a combination of numbers and letters. E-mail addresses always use lowercase letters with no spaces.

E-Mail Manager
Also called **mail reader**; a tool to manage e-mail and to communicate on the Internet. E-mail managers may be built into the communications software you are using. Your e-mail manager allows you to compose, read, reply, print, save, and delete mail messages.

Emoticons
A combination of symbols and letters usually sent with electronic mail that when combined display a little picture that expresses an emotion when you tilt your head to the left side. The most popular emoticon is the smiley, :-).

Encryption
Encoding sensitive information so that if it's intercepted a user without the proper key won't be able to understand it.

F

FAQ
Frequently Asked Question; refers to a page containing common questions about Internet services and their answers. This prevents individuals, newsgroup providers, and mailing list providers from

having to answer the same questions repeatedly. Always check the FAQ list before you post a question.

Favorites
A term used by the browser Microsoft Internet Explorer to flag the location of a document. (See *Bookmark*.)

File Extension
A suffix to a file name that further identifies the contents of the file. For example, DOG.GIF indicates that this is a graphic file. Other common file name extensions for graphics include .PCX, .TIF or .TIFF, .JPEG or .JPG, .PICT, and .BMP. (See *GIF* and *JPEG*.)

Firewall
A system of computer hardware and software that isolates a company's local area network from the Internet. The firewall is set up to protect the company's computers from potential tampering from Internet "hackers." Many companies with firewalls contract with Internet service providers to serve their World Wide Web pages.

Flame
An electronic mail message or newsgroup posting that is violently argumentative or intends to attack another user verbally.

FTP
File Transfer Protocol; an Internet tool that allows a user to retrieve and transfer a file from a computer anywhere on the Internet to another computer. FTP files include freeware or shareware programs,

publications, clip art, and many others. The address for FTP sites begins with *ftp*. (See *Anonymous FTP*.)

G

Gateway
A computer that acts as a connector between two physically separate networks. It has interfaces to more than one network and can translate the packets of one network to another possibly dissimilar network.

GIF
Graphic Interchange Format; a type of graphics file format ending with the extension *.GIF* and used extensively on the World Wide Web. (See *File Extension*.)

Gopher
A tool that allows you to search millions of directories and databases of text documents on the Internet through a series of hierarchical menus. Even though most people now use the World Wide Web instead of the gopher, some prefer the faster text-only gopher system. Gopher browsers cannot read World Wide Web pages. The address for Gopher sites begins with *gopher*.

gov
A top-level domain that means government. (See *Domain Extension*.)

Graphical Browser
A special software program, often called a GUI or a graphical user interface and pronounced *gooey*, that allows you to access text, color, video,

sound, and multimedia presentations on the Internet. Popular graphical browsers are Netscape Navigator and Microsoft Internet Explorer.

GUI
See *Graphical Browser*.

H

Home Page
The main page for a World Wide Web site. Often the home page is like an index and has links to other pages at this site. (See *Web Page*.)

Host
An Internet computer.

Hot List
A feature of a graphical browser that lists your bookmarks or favorite pages and allows you to access them quickly and easily. (See *Bookmark* and *Favorites*.)

HTML
HyperText Markup Language; refers to the embedded directions within regular text to create World Wide Web pages. These instructions allow a browser to display a document clearly on your screen. Some HTML documents have *.html* or *.htm* at the end of the URL.

HTTP
HyperText Transfer Protocol; the communications instructions used to connect World Wide Web sites across the Internet. The address for most World Wide Web documents begins with *http*.

Hypertext
A portion of a text document that contains programming code to link a word, graphic,

or phrase to another section in a document or to a different document. Hypertext links on home pages and web pages are highlighted, underlined, or in a different color.

I

Information Superhighway
Also called **cyberspace**; a term popularized by Vice President Al Gore in describing the National Information Infrastructure project. According to his vision, the information superhighway is a high-speed network of computers that will serve thousands of users simultaneously, transmitting e-mail, multimedia files, voice, and video. Its construction is being financed by private industry, primarily the telephone and cable companies. (See *Cyberspace*.)

Internet
Also called *Net*; the worldwide "network of networks" that connects networks to each other using the TCP/IP protocol. Connected networks can transfer files, send electronic mail, exchange newsgroups, and share information via clients such as the World Wide Web, Gopher, and FTP. (See *Client*, *FTP*, *Gopher*, and *World Wide Web*.)

Internet Address
See *E-Mail Address*.

Internet Service Provider
ISP; a company that provides full access to the Internet through a phone line. Many providers are now offering unlimited use dial-up connections to the Internet for reasonable monthly rates. You

must have a computer, communications software, and a modem with a phone line.

J

JPEG
A type of graphics file format (pronounced *jay peg*) ending with the extension *.JPEG* in which photographs are stored for viewing on the World Wide Web. This format compresses the size of a scanned photograph to use less disk space. (See *File Extension*.)

L

LAN
Local Area Network; a group of linked computers located within a specifically defined area such as an office or a building.

Links
See *Hypertext*.

Listserv
Also called a **mailing list**; an electronic discussion group that tends to be more academically focused than newsgroups. A listserv is composed of people who have voluntarily subscribed themselves to focus on a special interest topic. Thousands of listservs exist on all topics. You can join a listserv through your e-mail account.

Login
A procedure to identify yourself to the computer system that provides access to the Internet. Typically, this includes your user ID and password. (See *Logout*.)

Logout
Sometimes referred to as *log-off*; a procedure to inform a computer system that you are quitting your computer session. (See *Login*.)

Lurking
A term that refers to reading but not posting articles to a newsgroup.

Lynx
See *Text Browser*.

M

Mailing List
See *Listserv*.

Microsoft Internet Explorer
See *Graphical Browser*.

mil
A top-level domain that means military. (See *Domain Extension*.)

Modem
The hardware that transfers data by converting computer signals that can be transmitted over a telephone line. Most personal computers come with modems at the speed of 14.4 bps (bits per second) or 28.8 bps. (See *Bits per Second*.)

Multimedia
A combination of more than one medium, such as text, audio, video, graphics, animation, and images.

N

net
A top-level domain that means network provider. (See *Domain Extension*.)

Net
Another term for Internet. (See *Internet*.)

Netiquette
Network etiquette, or the unwritten and written "rules" of etiquette, to be observed when communicating on the Internet.

Netscape Navigator
See *Graphical Browser*.

Network
Two or more computers linked together so that they can exchange files and messages and share resources such as software, hardware, and data. Some large companies and institutions have networks that include thousands of computers.

Newsgroup
See *USENET*.

O

org
A top-level domain that means organization. (See *Domain Extension*.)

P

Password
A secret character string or word used to secure computer systems.

Post
To send or contribute articles to an electronic discussion such as a newsgroup or bulletin board system.

PPP
Point-to-Point Protocol; a type of protocol used to connect a computer to the Internet through a modem and telephone line. Internet service providers usually sell a PPP connection to home users or low-volume individual

business users. PPP is more powerful and dependable than the older SLIP method. (See *SLIP*.)

Protocol
An agreed-upon standard for electronic communications; a common language for computers. This allows users of Apples, PCs, and mainframe computers to communicate with each other over the Internet. (See *TCP/IP*.)

S

Search Engine
An Internet tool that allows you to search for information on a particular topic all across the Internet. After you type a keyword or phrase, the search engine will display documents in which the keyword appears. Popular search engines are Yahoo, AltaVista, Magellan, Lycos, and Excite.

Server
A computer that can provide resources, such as software, hardware, and data, for other computers to use.

Shareware
A method of software distribution in which computer programs are marketed and distributed electronically without proper licensing. The developer may request a registration fee if you decide to keep the software.

SLIP
Serial Line Internet Protocol; a type of protocol used to connect a computer to the Internet through a modem. In most cases, PPP has replaced SLIP. (See *PPP*.)

Snail Mail
A term used to refer to the slower speed of postal mail as contrasted to the faster speed of e-mail.

Subdomain
Each part of a domain. For example, in billg@microsoft.com, *microsoft* and *com* are subdomains in this e-mail address. (See *Domain*, *Domain Name System*, *E-Mail Address*, and *Username*.)

Subscribe
To join or sign up as a member of a newsgroup of listserv. (See *Listserv*, *Unsubscribe*, and *USENET*.)

T

T1 Line
A high-speed, dedicated connection to the Internet that allows hundreds of users to access the World Wide Web server simultaneously.

TCP/IP
Transmission Control Protocol/Internet Protocol; the name of the collection of rules used to connect computers and networks. As a result, one computer can communicate with any other computer on the Internet.

Telnet
The oldest Internet service that allows you to log in to another Internet computer. Telnet is not very common anymore as a means to download information.

TENET
Texas Education Network; a menu-based telecommunications network developed for Texas educators and students

through the Department of Information Resources, the Texas Education Agency, and The University of Texas. TENET provides a communication link to the Internet.

Text Browser
A special software program that provides access to only text (or words) on the Internet. For example, Lynx is a text browser. Lynx does not allow users to view graphics.

U

UNIX
The operating system on many original Internet computers. The UNIX operating system has pieces of basic Internet software built in which allow UNIX users to connect and use the Internet.

Unsubscribe
To cancel membership to a newsgroup or a listserv. (See *Listserv*, *Subscribe*, and *USENET*.)

Upload
To copy a file or information from your computer to another computer or server. (See *Download*.)

URL
Universal Resource Locator; the specific and unique address of a particular document, file, graphic, sound, or video on the World Wide Web.

USENET
Sometimes referred to as Netnews or Usenet News; a network that provides access to electronic discussion groups called newsgroups or conferences. Thousands of newsgroups exist on all topics to

which you can subscribe. With newsgroups you can exchange ideas, ask questions, offer options, or just lurk. The newsgroups to which you have access depend on the service your Internet service provider provides. (See *Internet Service Provider* and *Lurk*.)

Username
Part of an e-mail address that identifies the specific person at the site. For example, in billg@microsoft.com, *billg* is the username. (See *Domain*, *Domain Name Systems*, *E-Mail Address*, and *Subdomain*.)

W

WAIS
Wide Area Information Service; a means to access databases and libraries located on WAIS servers throughout the Internet. WAIS information searches are initiated by keywords and topics and can be compared to the index of a book.

Web Page
Also called **page**; contains the information for a hypertext link. (See *Home Page*.)

White Pages
A term used to reference a database (similar to a telephone book without phone numbers) that contains basic information about subscribers on a network, such as their name, e-mail address, telephone number, and postal address.

WWW
World Wide Web; a hypermedia system that lets you browse through related documents on the Internet through the use of hypertext links. (See *Hypertext*.)

Index